George Cary Eggleston

Southern Soldier Stories

George Cary Eggleston

Southern Soldier Stories

ISBN/EAN: 9783337135300

Printed in Europe, USA, Canada, Australia, Japan

Cover: Foto ©ninafisch / pixelio.de

More available books at **www.hansebooks.com**

J. E. B. Stuart.—The Cavalier.

Southern Soldier Stories

By

George Cary Eggleston

Author of "A Rebel's Recollections," etc., etc.

With Illustrations by R. F. Zogbaum

New York
The Macmillan Company
London: Macmillan & Co., Ltd.
1898

Norwood Press
J. S. Cushing & Co.—Berwick & Smith
Norwood Mass. U.S.A.

TO "JOE"

I DEDICATE THIS BOOK TO THE "JOE" SO OFTEN
MENTIONED IN THESE STORIES
HE WAS MY LOVED COMRADE IN ARMS, AND A
SHARER IN ALL MY WAR EXPERIENCES
HE IS NOW

Dr. Joseph W. Eggleston

OF RICHMOND, VIRGINIA

PREFACE

THE use of the first personal pronoun singular in any of these stories does not of necessity mean that the author had anything to do with the events chronicled.

"I tell the story as 'twas told to me."

CONTENTS

	PAGE
How Battles are Fought	1
Joe	7
Around the Camp-fire	11
An Unfinished Fight	18
A Family that had no Luck	22
William	25
A Cradle Captain	29
Who is Russell?	31
"Juanita"	48
Scruggs	52
Joe on Horseback	55
A Rather Bad Night	57
The Women of Petersburg	70
Ham Seay	74
Old Jones's Dash	76
A Woman's Hair	80
A Midnight Crime	85
A Little Rebel	90
Twenty-one	97
A Beef Episode	104
Bernard Poland's Prophecy	107
A Breach of Etiquette	121

Contents

	PAGE
The Lady of the Green Blind	124
Youngblood's Last Morning	128
Billy Goodwin	133
Manassas	137
My Last Night on Picket	143
Griffith's Continued Story	147
A Cheerful Supper of Cheers	155
How the Tar Heels Stuck	157
"Little Lamkin's Battery"	159
Curry	171
Gun-boats	175
Two Minutes	179
Si Tucker — Coward and Hero	182
War as a Therapeutic Agent	188
"Notes on Cold Harbor"	191
A Plantation Heroine	203
Two Incidents in Contrast	206
How the Sergeant-major told the Truth	210
Two Gentlemen at Petersburg	215
Old Jones and the Huckster	220
A Dead Man's Message	223
A Woman's Last Word	225
An Incomplete Story	228
Random Facts	231
My Friend Phil	237

ILLUSTRATIONS

J. E. B. Stuart — The Cavalier . .	*Frontispiece*
	FACING PAGE
"Get up here and do your duty"	30
A Good-bye to a Friend	56
She was singing "Dixie"	91
The last that was seen of Bernard Poland . .	119
A Dead Man's Message	224

SOUTHERN SOLDIER STORIES

HOW BATTLES ARE FOUGHT

A PREFATORY EXPLANATION FOR THE BENEFIT OF THOSE WHO KNOW NOTHING ABOUT THE MATTER

When squads or scouting parties meet each other, they either fight in an irregular fashion or they run away.

With a systematic battle it is different.

Before a systematic battle, one army selects some place at which to resist the advance of the other.

The advancing army usually cannot leave the other aside and go on by another route to the capital city which it wants to reach, because, if it did, the army left aside would quickly destroy what is called the advancing army's "communications."

To destroy these communications would be to cut off supplies of food, ammunition, and everything else necessary to an army.

The army which takes the defensive selects

some point that can be most easily defended, — some point where a river or a creek, or a line of hills, or something else, serves to give it the advantage in a fight.

The enemy must either attack that army there, and drive it out of its position, or it must "flank" it out, if it is itself to go forward.

To "flank" an army out of position is not merely to pass it by, which, as explained above, might be dangerous, but to seize upon some point or some road, the possession of which will compel that army to retire.

Thus, when General Lee could not be driven out of his works at Fredericksburg by direct attack, General Hooker marched his army up the river, and by crossing there placed himself nearer Richmond than General Lee was. This compelled General Lee to abandon his position at Fredericksburg, and to meet General Hooker in the open field; otherwise there would have been nothing to prevent General Hooker from going to Richmond, with a part of his greatly superior force, leaving the rest of it to check any operations Lee might have undertaken against his communications.

It is in some such fashion as this that every battle is brought about. One side is ever trying to get somewhere, and the other side is ever trying to prevent it from doing so. Incidentally, each army is trying to destroy the other.

When one army has planted itself in a position of its choice, and the other advances to attack it, this is what happens: —

The army that is standing still throws out lines of pickets in front to watch for the enemy's advance and report it.

The enemy, as he advances, also throws out a cloud of skirmishers to "feel" of the position and avoid traps and ambushes.

A line of battle often extends over several miles in length, covering all available ground for attack or defence.

Before the advancing general can determine against what part of his adversary's line to hurl his heaviest battalions, he must study the conditions along that line; namely, by means of his skirmishers.

In the same way the general who is awaiting attack tries to discover through his skirmishers what his enemy's plan of battle is, and at what points he most needs to concentrate his own men.

While awaiting this information he posts his men — cavalry, artillery, and infantry — wherever he thinks they will be most useful, having reference all the time to their rapid movement during the battle from one part of the line to another, as occasion may demand.

He also holds a considerable part of his army "in reserve." That is to say, he stations it at points a little in rear of the line of battle, from which he can order all or any part of it to any point where strength may be needed.

In a great battle, involving large bodies of troops, each corps or division commander must do in a smaller way what the general-in-chief does on a larger scale. Each has charge of the battle on a certain part of the line. Each must take care of things within his own jurisdiction, and be ready at a moment's notice to respond to the demand of the commanding general for troops with which to help out elsewhere.

These are the generalities. Let us now come to the battle itself.

When the skirmishers of the advancing army meet the skirmishers of the resisting army, there is apt to be some pretty hot fighting for a time, and sometimes the artillery is considerably involved in it. But this is not the real thing; it is a mere preliminary to the actual battle.

The army that is standing on the defensive holds its lines in position — every battery placed where it will do the most good, and every infantryman lying down and taking the utmost advantage of every tree stump, log, or inequality of the ground, to protect himself as much as possible.

The men on horseback are either in front with the skirmishers, minutely observing the strength and movements of the enemy, or, having finished that work, are thrown out at the two ends of the lines, called "flanks," to watch there for possible movements of the enemy that might be otherwise unobserved. They are within call of any part of the line where need of them may arise.

While the skirmishers are doing their work, the heaviest strain of war falls on the nerves of the men in line of battle.

They have nothing to do but wait.

They wait with the certain knowledge that in a few minutes the advancing army will throw men forward, and thus convert its skirmish line into a line of attack; while on their own side they know that their skirmish line, after making all of discovery that temporary resistance can accomplish, will fall back, and that then the crucial conflict will begin.

Then comes the uproar of battle, — the dust, the blood, the advance, the retreat, the shock of arms, the murderous volleys of the infantry, the thunder storm of artillery; in short, the final desperate conflict of determined men for the mastery, all of them directed by cool-headed commanders, sitting on their horses at points of vantage for observation, and directing a reinforcement here, a withdrawal of men there, the hurrying of artillery to one point, an onset of cavalry at another, and at a critical moment an up-and-at-them charge with the bayonets. That usually ends matters one way or the other at the point involved. For only two or three times in any war do men with fixed bayonets on one side actually meet in physical shock men armed with fixed bayonets on the other.

Wherever there is advantage on either side, the general commanding that side throws troops forward in as heavy masses as possible to make the most of it. If one line or the other be broken, every conceivable effort is made to convert the breach into victory. And if victory comes, the cavalry thunder forward in pursuit and in an endeavor to convert the enemy's defeat into rout.

This is only a general description. I hope that no old soldier on either side will read it. It is not intended for such as they. It is written *virginibus puerisque*, and for other people who don't know anything about the subject. It is printed here in the hope that it may enable such persons a little better to understand these stories of strenuous conflict.

JOE

JOE was very much in earnest at Pocotaligo, South Carolina, where a great little battle was fought on the 22d of October, 1862.

That is to say, Joe was not quite seventeen years old, was an enthusiastic soldier, and was as hot headed as a boy well can be.

We had two batteries and a few companies of mounted riflemen — three hundred and fifty-one men all told — to oppose the advance of five thousand. We had only the nature of the country, the impassability of the marshes, and the long high causeways to enable us to make any resistance at all.

Before the battle of Pocotaligo proper began, we went two miles below to Yemassee and there made a stand of half an hour.

Our battery, numbering fifty-four men, received the brunt of the attack.

Joe had command of a gun.

His men fell like weeds before a scythe. Presently he found himself with only three men left with whom to work a gun.

The other battery was that of Captain Elliot of South Carolina; and Captain Elliot had just been designated Chief of Artillery. Elliot's battery was really not in action at all. Joe seeing Captain Elliot, and being himself full of the enthusiasm which insists upon getting things done, appealed to the Chief of Artillery for the loan of some cannoneers with whom to work his gun more effectively. Captain Elliot declined. Thereupon Joe broke into a volley of vituperation, calling the captain and his battery cowards, and by other pet names not here to be reported.

I, being Joe's immediate chief, as well as his elder brother, commanded him to silence and ordered him back to his gun. There he stood for fifteen minutes astride a dead man and pulling the lanyard himself. At the end of that time we were ordered to retire to Pocotaligo.

Joe was flushed, powder grimed, and very angry; so angry that even I came in for a part of his displeasure. When I asked him, in order that I might make report for the section, how many shots he had fired, he blazed out at me: "How do I know? I've been killing Yankees, not counting shots."

"How many rounds have you left in your limber-chest, Joe?" I asked.

He turned up the lid of the chest, and replied: "Five."

"And the chest had fifty, hadn't it, when you went into action?"

"Of course."

"Then you fired forty-five, didn't you?"

"Oh, I suppose so, I don't know! Confound these technicalities, anyhow! I'm *fighting*, not counting! Do your own arithmetic!"

It wasn't a very subordinate speech for a sergeant to make to the commander of his section, but Joe was my brother, and I loved him.

At Pocotaligo he fought his gun with superb devotion and effect. But he remained mad all over and clear through till two o'clock that night. At that hour I was able to persuade him that he had been indiscreet in his remarks to the Chief of Artillery.

"Maybe I was," he said, grasping my hand; "but you're not to worry, old fellow; I'll stand the consequences, and you're the best that ever was."

Nevertheless I did worry, knowing that such an offence was punishable without limit in the discretion of a court-martial. It was scarcely sunrise the next morning when I appeared at Captain Elliot's headquarters. I had ridden for half an hour, I suppose, my mind all the time recalling a certain military execution I had seen; but this morning I imagined Joe in the rôle of victim. I had not slept, of course, and my nerves were all on edge.

I entered headquarters with a degree of trepidation which I had never felt before.

Captain Elliot was performing his ablutions as well as he could, with a big gourd for basin. He nodded and spoke with his head in the towel.

"Good fight, wasn't it? We have a lot of those fellows to bury this morning. Pretty good bag for three hundred and fifty-one of us, and it was mainly your battery's cannister that did it."

I changed feet and said, "Y—e—s."

I thought to myself that that was about the way *I* should take to "let a man down easy" in a hard case.

The captain carefully removed the soap from his ears, then turning to me said : "That's a *fighter*, that brother of yours."

"Yes," I replied; "but, captain, he is very young, very enthusiastic, and very hot-tempered; I hope — I hope you'll overlook — his — er — intemperateness and—"

"THUNDER, MAN, DO YOU SUPPOSE I'VE GOT ANY GRUDGE AGAINST A FELLOW THAT FIGHTS LIKE THAT?" roared the gallant captain.

As I rode back through the woods, it seemed to me about the brightest October morning that I had ever seen, even in that superb Carolina climate.

AROUND THE CAMP-FIRE

IT was a kind of off-night, the 23d of October, 1862, twenty-four hours after the battle of Pocotaligo, on the South Carolina coast.

We had to stop over there until morning, because the creek was out of its banks, and we couldn't get across without daylight. There were only about a dozen of us, and we had to build a camp-fire under the trees.

After supper we fell to talking, and naturally we talked of war things. There wasn't anything else to talk about then.

There was the long-legged mountaineer, with the deep voice, and the drawl in his speech which aided the suggestion that he kept his voice in his boots and had to pump it up when anything was to be said. Opposite him was the alert, rapid-speaking fellow, who had come in as a conscript and had made a superb volunteer, — a fellow who had an opinion ready made on every subject that could be mentioned, and who was accustomed to wind up most conversations with a remark so philosophical as to seem strangely out of keeping with the rest of the inconsequent things that he had said. Then there were the two mountaineers who never said anything because they never had anything to say. They had reached that point of intellectual development where the theory is accepted that there ought to be thought behind every utterance; and under this misapprehension they abstained from utterance.

Joe was there, but Joe wasn't talking that night. Joe was surly and sullen. He had had to kill his horse at Pocotaligo the day before, and all the honors he had harvested from that action had not reconciled him to the loss. The new horse he had drawn was, in his opinion, "a beast." Of course all horses are beasts, but that isn't precisely what Joe meant. Besides, he had received a letter from his sweetheart just before we left camp, — she's his wife now, and the mother of his dozen or more children, — in which that young woman had expressed doubts as to whether, after all, he was precisely the kind of man to whom she ought to "give her life." Joe was only seventeen years of age at that time, and he minded little things like that. Still again, Joe had the toothache. Besides that, we were hungry after our exceedingly scant meal of roasted sweet potatoes. Besides that, it was raining.

All the circumstances contributed to make us introspective and psychological in our conversation.

The long-legged mountaineer with the deep voice was telling some entirely inconsequent story about somebody who wasn't known to any of us, and none of us was listening. After a while he said: "He was that sort of a feller that never felt fear in his life."

From Joe: "There never was any such fellow."

The long mountaineer: "Well, that's what he *said*, anyhow."

From Joe: "He lied, then."

"Well," continued the long-legged mountaineer, "that's what he said, and he sort o' lived up to it. If he had any fear, he didn't show it till that time I was tellin' you about, when he went all to pieces and showed the white feather."

"There," growled Joe, "what did I tell you? He was lying all the time."

The postscript philosopher on the other side of the fire broke in, saying: "Well, maybe his breakfast went bad on him that morning. An overdone egg would make a coward out of the Duke of Wellington."

Joe made the general reflection that "some people locate their courage in their transverse colons."

"What's a transverse colon?" asked one of the mountaineers. Joe got up, stretched himself, and made no answer. Perhaps none was expected.

"Well," asked the long-legged mountaineer, "ain't they people that don't feel no fear?"

The glib little fellow quickly responded: "Let's find out. Let's hold an experience meeting. I suppose we're a pretty fairly representative body, and I move that each fellow tells honestly how he feels when he is going into battle; for instance, when the skirmishers are at work in front, and we know that the next two minutes will bring on the business."

"Infernally bad," growled Joe; "and anybody that pretends to feel otherwise lies."

The postscript philosopher replied: "I never saw *you* show any fear, Joe."

"That's because I'm too big a coward to show it," said Joe.

Even the two reticent mountaineers understood that.

One of them was moved to break the silence. At last he had, if not a thought, yet an emotion to stand sponsor for utterance.

"*I* always feel," said he, "as though the squegees had took hold of my knees. There ain't anything of me for about a minute — exceptin' a spot in the small of my back. I always wish I was a woman or a baby, or dead or something like that. After a while I git holt of myself and I says to myself, 'Bill, you've got to stand up to the rack, fodder or no fodder.' After that it all comes sort of easy like, you know, because the firin' begins, and after the firin' begins you're doin' somethin', you see, and when you're fightin' like, things don't seem so bad. I s'pose you've all *noticed* that."

From Joe: "In all the works on psychology it has been recognized as a universal principle, that the mind when occupied with a superior consideration is able to free itself from considerations of a lesser sort."

The mountaineer looked at him helplessly and said nothing.

The postscript philosopher began: "I shall never forget my first battle. It wasn't much of a battle either, but it was lively while it lasted. Unfortunately for me it was one of those fights where you have to wait for the enemy to begin. I was tender then. I had just left home, and every time I looked at the little knickknacks mother and the girls had given me to make camp life comfortable, — for bless my soul they thought we *lived* in camp, — every time I looked at these things I grew teary. There oughtn't to be any bric-à-brac of that kind given to a fellow when he goes into the army. It isn't fit. It worries him."

He was silent for a minute. So were the rest of us. We all had bric-à-brac to remember. He resumed:

"We were lying there in the edge of a piece of woods with a sloping meadow in front, crossed by a stone wall heavily overgrown with vines. At the other edge of the meadow was another strip of woods. The enemy were somewhere in there. We knew they were coming, because the pickets had been driven in, and we stood there waiting for them. The waiting was the worst of it, and as we waited I got to feeling in my pockets and — pulled out a little, old three-cornered pincushion. Conscience knows I wouldn't have pulled out that pincushion at that particular minute to have won a battle. I've got it now. I never had any use for a pincushion because I never could pin any two things together the way a woman can, but a man can't make his womenkind believe that: I've kept it all through the war, and when I go back home — if it suits the Yankees that I ever go back at all — I'm going to give it as a souvenir to the little sister that made it for me. And I'm going to tell her that it was that pincushion, little three-cornered thing that it is, that made a man out of me that day.

"My first thought as I pulled it out was that I wanted to go home and give the war up; but then came another kind of a thought. I said, 'The little girl wouldn't have given that pincushion to me if she hadn't understood that I was going off to fight for the country.' So I said to myself, 'Old boy, you've got to stand your hand pat.' And now whenever we go into battle I always brace myself up a little by feeling in my breeches pocket and sort of shaping out that pincushion."

From Joe: "It's a good story, but the rest of us haven't any pincushions. Besides that, it's raining." I couldn't help observing that Joe drew that afternoon's letter out of his pocket and fumbled it a little, while the long-legged mountaineer was straightening out his limbs and his thoughts for his share in the conversation. He said in basso profundo: "The fact is I'm always so skeered just before a fight that I can't remember afterwards how I did feel. I know only this much, that that last three minutes before the bullets begin to whistle and the shells to howl, takes more out of me than six hours straightaway fightin' afterwards does."

From Joe: "There must be a lot in you at the start, then."

There were still two men unheard from in the experience meeting. Some one of us called upon them for an expression of opinion.

"I donno. I never thought," said one.

"Nuther did I," said the other.

"Of course you didn't," said Joe.

Then the postscript philosopher, rising and stretching himself, remarked: "I reckon that if any man goes into a fight without being scared, that man is drunk or crazy."

Then we all lay down and went to sleep.

AN UNFINISHED FIGHT

JACK SWAN was the best swordsman in the regiment — probably the best in the army. Jack was a Marylander, who came south singing " My Maryland," and heartily believing in the assertion of that song that

> " She breathes, she burns, she'll come, she'll come, Maryland, my Maryland!"

Like most men from border states he represented a house divided against itself. In his case the division was peculiarly distressing.

He was an enthusiastic Southerner. His twin brother was an equally enthusiastic Union man. The one was in the one army as a matter of conscience, and the other in the other for precisely the same reason. It was always a grief to Jack that this separation had come between him and the curly-headed twin brother, with whom he had slept in infancy, and who had been his comrade until that terrible fratricidal war had parted them.

He used to talk with us about it around the camp-fire, and was especially sad over it when any of us managed to get off for a day or a week to visit our homes. His home was beyond the lines; and in all that country for which he was fighting there was no human being whom he could call kin.

He had this comfort, however, that his brother and he were never likely to meet in the conflict of arms. For to avoid that the brother had betaken himself to the West and was serving in Mississippi. But there was always the terrible chance that in the shifting of troops they two might some day, unknown to each other, be fighting on opposite sides of the same field. That, in fact, is what happened at Brandy Station, and it happened more dramatically than either of the brothers had anticipated.

The conflict at Brandy Station was perhaps the greatest cavalry fight of the war. It was the one contest in which large bodies of armed and trained horsemen, under the greatest cavalry leaders on either side, met fairly in conflict with little or no interference from troops of other arms.

It was the only contest of the kind, so far as I know, in which highly expert swordsmen met each other fairly in single combat. There was on both sides a chivalric feeling akin to that of the "knights of old," which prompted men not to interfere when two well-matched cavaliers met each other with naked blades.

Jack Swan was naturally eager for a fray of

this sort. He knew and mightily rejoiced in his superb skill with the sabre.

He watched anxiously for his opportunity. Presently it came.

A singularly lithe young fellow from one of the Northern regiments met and slew, in the open field, one of our officers. Thereupon Jack turned to his captain and said: "If I have your leave, captain, I'd like to try conclusions with that young fellow myself. He seems to know how to handle sharp steel."

The captain nodded assent, and Jack put spurs to his horse. The two men met in midfield. They crossed swords as a couple of gladiators might, while a thousand eyes watched anxiously for the result.

It was manifestly to be a contest of experts, a battle of the giants, for both men were above the average in height and weight, and both knew every trick of the sabre.

Their swords drew fire from each other's edge at the first onset.

Then they paused strangely and looked at each other. Then Jack deliberately threw his sabre upon the ground and uncovered his head.

His adversary could have run him through on the instant, but the action of Jack seemed to give him pause. He stopped with his sword poised at the tierce thrust. He leant forward eagerly and gazed into the calm eyes of the

Confederate. Then he, too, abandoning his purpose, threw his weapon to the ground.

We were all eagerness and curiosity; and neither our eagerness nor our curiosity was relieved when the two men grasped each other's hand, swung their horses around, and each returned unarmed to his own line.

When Jack rode up he had just six words of explanation to make.

"That man," he said, "is my twin brother."

That seemed to be all there was to say. "Blood is thicker than water."

A FAMILY THAT HAD NO LUCK

THERE were two instances of supreme heroism in the Civil War. One was upon the one side, the other upon the other.

One was the charge of Pickett's Southerners at Gettysburg. The other was the heroic series of assaults, made by the Northern troops on Marye's Heights, at Fredericksburg.

General Lee's works in the last-named battle were high up on the hill. Crossing the field in front of them was a sunken road — a perfect breastwork already formed. The main body of the army was in the works above; but a multitude of us were thrown forward into the sunken road.

The enemy knew nothing of this geographical peculiarity. But their first advance revealed the impossibility of breaking Lee's lines at that point. The column that advanced was swept away as with a broom before it got within firing distance of the works it supposed itself to be attacking. The men knew what that meant. Wiser than their general, they saw the necessity of selecting some other point of attack. Nevertheless when their commander persisted, they six times came unflinchingly to an assault which every man of them knew to be hopeless. This may not have been war, but it was heroism.

We who faced them there honored it as such.

Just as we tumbled into the sunken road, an old man came in bearing an Enfield rifle and wearing an old pot hat of the date of 1857 or thereabouts. With a gentle courtesy that was unusual in war, he apologized to the two men between whom he placed himself, saying: "I hope I don't crowd you, but I must find a place somewhere from which I can shoot."

At that moment one of the great assaults occurred. The old man used his gun like an expert. He wasted no bullet. He took aim every time and fired only when he knew his aim to be effective. Yet he fired rapidly. Tom Booker, who stood next to him, said as the advancing column was swept away: "You must have shot birds on the wing in your time."

The old man answered: "I did up to twenty year ago; but then I sort o' lost my sight, you know, and my interest in shootin'."

"Well, you've got 'em both back again," called out Billy Goodwin from down the line.

"Yes," said the old man. "You see I had to. It's this way: I had six boys and six gells. When the war broke out I thought the six boys could do my family's share o' the fightin'. Well, they did their best, but they didn't have no luck.

One of 'em was killed at Manassas, two others in a cavalry raid, and the other three fell in different actions — 'long the road as you might say. We ain't seemed to a had no luck. But it's just come to this, that if the family is to be represented, the old man must git up his shootin' agin, or else one o' the gells would have to take a hand. So here I am."

Just then the third advance was made. A tremendous column of heroic fellows was hurled upon us, only to be swept away as its predecessors had been. Two or three minutes did the work, but at the end of that time the old man fell backward, and Tom Booker caught him in his arms.

"You're shot," he said.

"Yes. The family don't seem to have no luck. If one o' my gells comes to you, you'll give her a fair chance to shoot straight, won't you, boys?"

WILLIAM

IT was during the long waiting time.
The battle of Manassas had been fought in July, and for months afterward, there was nothing for us to do. We had failed to assail Washington, and the enemy was not yet sufficiently recovered from his demoralization — the completest that ever overcame an army — to assail us.

We had time, therefore, to quarrel among ourselves.

Two men had met in a glade in a thicket some distance from the camp. They were taking their quarrel very seriously, and had met to fight it out without the formality of seconds or other familiar frills of the duello. They crossed sabres.

It was then that Billy Gresham broke through the bushes and interposed.

Billy was a recognized "character." He was a phenomenal egotist, but he rarely used the first personal pronoun singular. Instead of saying "I" or "me," he usually said "William." But he said it with an unctuousness and appreciation of its significance that cannot be described in words.

Also Billy Gresham always did what he pleased, without a thought of having to give an account of his conduct to anybody. His extraordinary loquacity was a perfect safeguard against any possible challenge of resentment. He could talk anybody down and close the conversation at his own sweet will. The worst that his adversary could do was to laugh at him, and Billy didn't mind that in the least. He regarded it rather as a grateful tribute to his humor.

Just as the two men crossed swords, Billy broke through the bushes, and interposed his blade — with a very good imitation of stage heroism — between the combatants. Then, with all the authority of an expert in a matter he knew nothing about, he proceeded to lay down laws of his own extemporaneous invention for the governance of single combat.

"Stop, gentlemen!" he cried out. Then, laying his sword on the ground between them, he said: "You must not cross my sword with yours, gentlemen. To do that would be to put an affront upon William which only blood could efface, and it must be the blood of the offender — not the gore of private William Gresham."

The two men had come to a pause, of course. Equally of course, they were smiling at the ridiculousness of Billy Gresham's interference and the absurdity of his chatter.

Still their purpose to fight remained in undiminished intensity. Seeing this, Billy resumed his talk.

"If you are determined to fight," he said, "you can do so. Far be it from William to interrupt a prearranged engagement for mutual dissection between two of his friends. But William always likes to have a little money up on the probabilities."

Then pulling out a pocket-book, which was fat with humorous newspaper clippings, but which both men knew to contain nothing more valuable, he caressed it lovingly and said: "Before you proceed, William wants to bet one hundred dollars to ten with one or both of you — you can make it a thousand dollars to a hundred, if you prefer — that neither of you two sublimated idiots can give William a reasonable excuse for this quarrel. Come now, before you enter upon the business of mutual slaughter, make a bet that will provide in some degree for the loved ones dependent on you."

By that time both men were laughing, for, after all, their quarrel was a trifling one. They would not have quarrelled at all if the intensity of the nervous strain put upon them by the war had been relieved by active duty.

"Now," said Billy, "William has another bet to make. He offers a hundred to one that if the colonel catches you fellows at this sort of idiotic performance, he'll take the 'honor' out of both of you by making you grub stumps for weeks to come. Put up your swords and shake hands, or else take the bets."

The absurdity of the situation ended it. Billy remarked: "Now let William give you a tip. There is the enemy to fight; and if William does not hopelessly misunderstand the temper of George B. McClellan's army, they will give us all the fighting we want without anything of this sort."

It was Billy who, at the end of the war, protested his loyalty to the Southern cause by vowing that he would never send a letter unless it could go under cover of a Southern postage-stamp. I am credibly informed that for thirty odd years he has kept this vow.

It must have spared him a great deal of trouble.

A CRADLE CAPTAIN

THEY said we had robbed the cradle and the grave to recruit our army.
We had.
The cradle contingent acquitted itself particularly well.

He was a very little fellow. He was said to be fourteen years old. He didn't look it. In his captain's uniform he suggested the need of a nurse with cap and apron. But when it came to doing the work of a soldier the impression was different.

It was in 1864, late summer. We were in the trenches outside a fortification engaged in bombarding Fort Harrison, below Richmond. The enemy had captured that work, and it was deemed necessary to drive him out. To that end we had been sent from Petersburg to the north side of James River, with twenty-two mortars to rain a hundred shells a minute into the fort preparatory to the infantry charge.

A gun-boat had been ordered up the river to help in the bombardment. The gun-boat mistook *us* for Fort Harrison and opened upon our defenceless rear. Its shells were about the size and shape of a street lamp, and they wrought fearful havoc among us.

The Cradle Captain had charge of the signal operator — a stalwart mountaineer of six feet four or so.

The Cradle Captain ordered him to mount upon the glacis and signal the ship to cease firing. The man was not a coward; but the fire was terrific. He hesitated. That Cradle Captain leaped like a cat upon the glacis, which the shells were splitting every second. He pulled out two pistols. He presented one at each side of the mountaineer's head. Then in a little, childish, piping voice he said: "Get up here and do your duty, or I'll blow your brains out."

We rejoiced that the lead, which at that moment laid the little soldier low, came from the enemy's guns, and not from our own mistaken comrades. The Cradle Captain was glad, too, for as he was carried away on a litter, he laughed out between groans: "It wasn't our men that did it, for I had made that hulking idiot get in that signal all right, anyhow."

"GET UP HERE AND DO YOUR DUTY."

WHO IS RUSSELL?

I SAW him for the first time in 1862.
We were stationed on the coast of South Carolina, and never was there an idler set of soldiers than we.

We were in the midst of a great war, it is true, and ours was a fighting battery with dates on its battle banner; but on the coast we had literally nothing to do. The position of our camp was determined by military geography, and it could not be changed. A fight was possible any day, and now and then a fight came. But we knew in advance precisely where it must be waged, and until our foemen chose to bring it about, we had no occasion for marching or bivouacking. They were on the sea islands. We were on the mainland. We had no means of crossing to the islands. They could cross to the mainland whenever they pleased. When they came, it was our business to meet them and keep them from reaching the line of railroad along the coast.

Every little stream and every little inlet was bordered by an impassable morass, which could be crossed only by way of a high and narrow causeway. The places where the roads crossed the streams were, therefore, the predestined battlefields. We were stationed with reference to these crossings.

We idled away the time, and like all idle people near a small railroad station we knew of the comings and goings of everybody in the country roundabout.

Everybody, that is to say, except Russell.

His coming was a mystery. In fact, he did not come at all. He simply appeared one evening as a looker-on at roll-call.

There was no way by which he could have come to Pocotaligo except by train; and we knew that he had not come by train. The whole body of us regularly attended the incoming of every train, and promptly pumped all the news out of every arriving passenger.

Russell had not come by train. Therefore Russell had not come at all. Yet there he was.

He was a comely young fellow. So shapely were his limbs and so exact the proportions of his frame that no one, without a second look at him, would have realized his symmetry, his extraordinary strength, or his activity. His head was a study for the sculptor. In limbs, torso, features, complexion, and bearing he stood there in the Southern sunset a very model of manly beauty.

When the roll-call was ended, he came up to

me, and, touching his hat gracefully, introduced himself.

"My name is William Russell. I shall be obliged if you will let me remain with your men over night. I shall probably ask to enlist to-morrow."

His words were simple enough, and his manner was that of a modest gentleman; but there was that in his voice that fascinated me beyond measure. Had any other stranger come up to me with a like request, I should have questioned him closely, and possibly have turned him over for the night to the hospitality of one of the messes. With Russell I did nothing of the sort. He was a gentleman visiting our camp. I could do no less than invite him to sup and lodge with me. He had sought no such hospitality, but when I offered it, he frankly accepted it.

I found him to be a particularly agreeable guest. He talked fluently, but modestly, on all subjects as they arose. Before my brother officers came into my quarters for our nightly game of whist, I had discovered that Russell was not only a man of broad general education, but one thoroughly familiar with English, German, and French literature as well. We learned very indirectly that he had travelled extensively, and that travel had wrought in him its perfect work in making him an agreeable companion.

The next morning he expressed a wish to enlist with us. He persisted in this, in spite of our assurances that our rude, uncultivated mountaineers were not fit companions for him.

After his enlistment he carefully avoided everything like presumption upon our previous hospitality, or upon his own evident superiority. He knew the distinction between officers and enlisted men, and he observed it with a rigidity wholly unknown in our rather democratic service. I was glad sometimes to seek him out when I wanted a companion, and on such occasions he responded promptly to my invitations, but he never once came to my quarters, or those of any other officer, uninvited.

He was always quiet and modest, and it was only by accident that we learned little by little how many and varied his accomplishments were. It was not only that he never boasted; he was even shy of letting us find out for ourselves how many things he could do surprisingly well.

The men had built a number of gymnastic structures, and of afternoons their contests of strength and skill were attended by everybody in the neighborhood. For more than a month Russell looked on as a casually interested spectator. One afternoon, however, some of our best gymnasts were trying to accomplish a new and rather difficult feat. When they were ready to abandon the attempt as hopeless, Russell modestly said to the most persistent one among them: "I think if you will reverse the position of your hands you can do that."

The man reversed his hands, but awkwardly.

"Not that way; let me show you," said Russell. And going to the bars he quickly did the thing himself with no apparent exertion whatever. Then, as if in mere wantonness of strength and skill, he went rapidly through a series of gymnastic feats of the most difficult sort imaginable, ending the performance with a number of somersaults that would have done honor to an acrobat. When he had done, we all clapped hands and shouted our applause. Russell simply blushed as a woman might and went to his hut.

I never knew him to touch the bars again, so averse was he to anything like display.

When I ventured to ask him in private one day how and where he had acquired his skill, he replied: "Oh, I have no skill to speak of in the matter. It's merely a trick or two I picked up at a German university."

In this way we learned one thing after another about the man, though he vouchsafed us no information concerning his past history, except so much as we had discovered in mustering him into service. That consisted of but one fact: that William Russell was born in Kentucky;

and that isolated fact was a falsehood, as Russell afterwards informed me.

One day, some months after his enlistment, there was an explosion in camp.

A chief of caisson had been tinkering with a shell from the enemy's camp which had not burst. It exploded in his hands, literally blowing one of them off midway between the wrist and the elbow. When I came to the poor fellow he was lying on the ground, the blood spurting from the severed artery.

The surgeon and all my brother officers had ridden away, no one knew whither, and I was completely at a loss to know what to do. Before I had time to decide anything, Russell pushed his way through the throng, drew out his handkerchief, knotted it, and quickly tightened it around the man's arm.

"Will you please hold that steadily?" said he in the calmest possible voice to one of the excited men. Then turning to me and touching his cap, he said: "Will you allow me to go to the surgeon's quarters for some necessary things? I think I may help this poor fellow."

"Certainly," I replied, "if you can do anything for him, do it by all means."

He walked rapidly, but without a sign of excitement, to the hospital tent, and returned almost immediately with some bottles, bandages, and a case of instruments.

Turning to me he said: "Will you do me the favor to put your finger on the corporal's pulse and observe its beating carefully? If it sinks or becomes irregular, please let me know immediately."

With that he saturated a handkerchief with chloroform, and using a peremptory form of speech for the first time in my experience of him, he ordered one of the men to hold it to the wounded corporal's nose.

"What are you going to do?" I asked in astonishment.

"I am going to amputate this man's arm, if you have no objection," he returned, as he opened the case of instruments. And he did amputate it in a most skilful manner, as the surgeon testified on his return. The operation over, Russell gave minute directions for the care of the wounded man.

My astonishment may well be imagined. The men, however, were not surprised. Their faith in Russell was unbounded already. They had so often seen him do as an expert things that nobody had imagined him capable of doing at all, that they had come to think him equal to any emergency, as indeed it seemed that he was.

For myself, I am free to confess that my curiosity was sharply piqued. I determined to question Russell in detail about himself and his past at the first opportunity. When the opportunity came, however, the man's modest dignity so impressed me that I could not bring myself to do anything so rude and discourteous. I contented myself with saying: "Why, Russell, I didn't know you were a surgeon?"

"I can hardly claim to be that," he replied, "though I gave some little attention to the subject while I was abroad."

It then occurred to me to suggest the propriety of his asking for a surgeon's commission, as it really seemed a pity that a man so accomplished as he should remain a private in a company made up almost entirely of illiterate mountaineers. He refused to entertain the idea for a moment, saying: "I am entirely contented with my lot and do not care to change."

One day, not long after this occurrence, I was playing at chess with Russell. Apropos of something or other, I told him an anecdote illustrative of Japanese character.

"Pardon me," he replied, "but you are misinformed," and straightway he proceeded to tell me many interesting facts with regard to the Orientals, all of which were evidently the result of personal observation. I presently discovered, as I thought, that Russell had been an officer in the United States navy, and that he had gone to Japan with Commodore Perry's expedition.

When a month or two later our battery was

sent to a little place immediately on the water, and a good deal of boat service was expected of us, our first care was to train our mountaineers in the use of oars and sails. With the exception of Russell, Joe, and myself, not a man in the battery knew the difference between a mast and a keel. It was determined, therefore, to divide the company into boat's crews for drill, and to make of Russell chief drill sergeant.

When the order providing for this was read on parade, Russell said nothing. But I had hardly reached my quarters before he came, cap in hand, asking to see me in private.

"I must beg you to excuse me from this boat-drill duty; I really can't do it."

"But you must," I returned. "The men must be taught to handle the boats, and your skill and experience are quite indispensable."

"But I have no skill or experience in the matter," he replied. "The truth is I do not even know the nomenclature of a boat. I do know the bow from the rudder, but that is the extreme limit of my knowledge on the subject."

This, from an ex-naval officer, was certainly rather odd, but I could not bring myself to question this modest gentleman further on the subject, or even to suspect his veracity, in which I had learned to repose the most implicit confidence.

He was not at all averse to boating duty in

itself. On the contrary, when an oar was put into his hands, his supple muscles lent themselves with a will to the severe physical strain. The man seemed even to rejoice in the opportunity thus given him to bring his magnificent strength into play. When his fellows quitted the boats in utter weariness he, still fresh, would betake himself to a little shell and row her about for hours in mere wantonness of unexpended vitality.

But he knew nothing of boating. He was as awkward as possible at first. He learned rapidly, however, and soon became a graceful oarsman and an expert sailor.

I was puzzled. I could not reconcile the man's stories of naval service with his evident ignorance of everything pertaining to a boat. Yet I could not doubt the truthfulness of any of his statements. Nobody who knew his gentleness, his modesty, and his translucent integrity as I did could possibly entertain doubt of his truthfulness. The man's face was of itself a certificate of his entire trustworthiness. His conduct and his manners were unexceptionable always. The man himself was the embodiment of truth.

Accordingly, when I observed some tattoo marks on his arm one day, which he told me were put there while he was in the navy, it did not occur to me to question him as to the truth of that story. On the contrary, I thought at the moment of a possible explanation of the whole matter: Perhaps he had been a surgeon in the service, and if so his technical ignorance of boating was not altogether unaccountable. I was surprised, however, to see that the letters on his arm were not " W. R." but " W. W." — a fact of which he volunteered an explanation.

"My name is not Russell," he said, "but Wallace. Though for a good many years I have preferred to use my mother's rather than my father's name."

As a matter of course I asked him no rude questions. He was altogether too much a gentleman for me to think of such a thing. I accepted his explanation and respected his wish to be called "Russell" still. He imposed no pledge of secrecy upon me, but I kept his secret sacredly, respecting it as a confidential communication from one gentleman to another.

I had hardly settled it in my own mind that Russell's connection with the navy had been in the capacity of a surgeon, when he came one day with the request that he might be allowed to go to Charleston for the purpose of standing an examination for admission to the navy as an officer.

This time, I confess, I was astonished. And so I went with him to Charleston and before the board. To my surprise, he passed his examination so brilliantly, that he was commissioned at once and put in command of a newly built gun-boat. Shortly afterwards he handled his vessel so well in a fight off the harbor as to secure an official compliment and a promotion.

About a week after that event I learned that he had deserted the navy and was among the missing. Apparently the poor fellow was a man running away from his past, and nothing was so disastrous to him as distinction.

I thus lost sight of Russell, and until August, 1873, I heard no more of him. I was editing a weekly family newspaper in New York at that time, and oddly enough I was just beginning to write this sketch of my singular acquaintance when Russell himself walked into my office at 245 Broadway and asked me if I remembered him. He was well dressed, in a quiet drab suit, and was scarcely at all changed. He told me that he was married and was living at a certain number in West 43d Street; that he was practising law, being senior member of the firm of Wintermute and Russell, for that his real name was Wintermute, and that his partner, Russell, was a cousin on the mother's side.

He gave me the firm's card, and begged me to call upon him, both at his house and at his office, which of course I promised to do.

I called first at the house. It was a well-built one of pressed brick, and seemed to wear something of Russell's own air of quiet dignity, standing as it did in a row of more pretentious brown-stone mansions. The door-plate — for door-plates were then still in use — bore the simple word, "Wintermute."

"Is Mr. Wintermute at home?" I asked.

"Commander Wintermute is in his library," answered the lackey, laying special stress upon the naval title.

"Ah, certainly, Commander Wintermute," I answered. "I had forgotten. Will you give him my card? I am an old friend."

I was shown into the parlor, — a conspicuously tasteful apartment, — furnished exactly as I should have expected Russell to furnish it.

After a little the door opened, and an elderly gentleman, obviously English, entered, holding my card in a puzzled way before his spectacled nose.

"Pardon me," he said. "The servant must have misunderstood you. He announced you as an old friend."

"Yes," I replied, "I asked for Commander Wintermute."

"I am he," replied the gentleman. "Though I certainly fail to recognize either your name or your face. There must be a mistake."

"There certainly seems to be," I answered, "unless there is another gentleman in your family. The one I am seeking is William Wintermute, whose mother's name was Russell."

"Then I am certainly the man," responded my companion. "My name is William Wintermute and my mother's name was Russell. There is no other gentleman living in the house, and so far as I have ever heard there is no other William Wintermute anywhere."

There was nothing to be done except to apologize and take my leave, which I did as gracefully as I could under the circumstances.

At last I was angry with Russell. I had been puzzled by him often enough. This time I was filled with resentment.

I at once sought out the law office of Wintermute and Russell. The card, which I had preserved, gave me all necessary information as to its whereabouts, and I was not long in finding it. Mr. Wintermute was there. So was Mr. Russell. But neither was the man for whom I was looking. Neither had ever heard of him.

I was still left puzzling over these questions:—
Who is Russell?
Is he after all a liar?
Or is he merely a remarkable coincidence?

* * * * *

In June or July, 1874, I published the foregoing sketch in a little monthly magazine printed in an obscure college town in Illinois, which had a circulation of only a few hundred copies, and lived just five months in all.

It was called the *Midland Monthly Magazine*, and was issued by a student in the college at Monmouth, Illinois.

Everything that related to Russell was sure in some way to blossom out with all sorts of strange coincidences. This did so. In spite of the obscure way in which my account of the man was published, I had no doubt whatever that it would sooner or later result in some new revelation of or concerning him.

It did so, of course.

The obscure student's magazine somehow found its way to Bordentown, New Jersey, and into the hands of an editor there. The editor was impressed by the story and reprinted it. It thus fell into the hands of the Reverend Lansing Burroughs, pastor of the First Baptist Church of that town, and late captain of Confederate States Artillery.

I was not surprised when I received from the Reverend Lansing Burroughs, etc., the following letter : —

BORDENTOWN, N. J., Sept. 5, 1874.

MY DEAR SIR : I have just finished reading a sketch published over your name (copied from somewhere, I suppose) in our local paper, entitled "Who is Russell ?" It petrifies me with astonishment. For thirteen years past the question which has bothered me most seriously has been, "Who is Russell?" alias "Wallace," alias "Wintermute," for by all these and some other names have I known the mysterious individual. If you have been writing only a fancy sketch, I must tackle one of the strangest problems in mental philosophy. If your story is one of experience, then must I see you and compare notes. I fancy I can horrify you with the story of what Russell once told me had been his history. . . .

Yours very truly,
LANSING BURROUGHS,
Pastor of the First Baptist Church, Bordentown, N. J.
Late captain Confederate States Artillery.

Now it was just like Russell that an account of him, published in a short-lived magazine, of a purely local circulation, out in Illinois, should in some inscrutable way have fallen into the hands of the editor of a little country paper in New Jersey; that this editor should have copied it into his paper; and that one of his readers should happen to be the one other man in existence who was puzzling over the questions with which the sketch ended.

But this was not all. There was still another coincidence. There was that in my correspondent's letter which revealed to me a fact of which he was apparently unconscious; namely, that this Reverend Lansing Burroughs was an old college mate of my own, whom I had not seen or heard from for sixteen years. Such a coincidence was altogether natural and proper, however, growing as it did out of matters connected with Russell.

I had some further correspondence with the Reverend Mr. Burroughs, and finally we met by appointment and went to Mouquin's for luncheon and to compare notes. A careful analysis of dates proved beyond doubt that *his* Russell was *my* Russell. But our experiences were of a very different sort. Mr. Burroughs had never once had a meeting with the mysterious man which did not bring calamity of some sort upon himself. So far as I was concerned, no ill beyond annoyance and embarrassment had ever come of my acquaintance with him.

The Reverend Mr. Burroughs declares to me his firm conviction that the quiet, singularly shy, well-behaved, modest gentleman, so unusually gifted, especially in the way of a phenomenal genius for lying, is in plain terms THE DEVIL.

As to this, Mr. Burroughs is by profession an expert, and I am not. I therefore venture no opinion. I merely continue to ask, "Who is Russell?"

"JUANITA"

I WAS on guard one night in the autumn of 1861.

It was only ordinary camp guard and not picket duty.

We had fallen back from the line of Mason's and Munson's hills, and were camped well in the rear of Fairfax Court House, which now constituted our most advanced outpost.

The army were fortified at Centreville. We had got tired of waiting for McClellan to make the advance for which we were so eagerly ready. We were evidently preparing to go into winter quarters.

We of Stuart's cavalry were still posted six or eight miles in advance of the main army; but after our summer, passed twenty miles in front, we felt snug and comfortable at "Camp Cooper."

Nevertheless, when I saw three rockets — red, white, and blue — go up far to the front, it occurred to me that the fact might mean something.

At any rate, I was lonely on post. I had

sung "Juanita" under my breath, — and that it wasn't permitted to sing out loud on post was probably a rule not made with any invidious reference to my voice, though it might well have been, — I say I had sung "Juanita" under my breath till I had exhausted the capabilities of entertainment that reside in that tender musical composition.

So, for the sake of diversion, if for nothing else, I called out: "Corporal of the guard, post number six."

When the corporal came and I reported what I had seen, he moodily growled something about there being no orders to "report on Yankee fireworks." Nevertheless, he communicated my report to higher authority.

Fifteen minutes later a hurried messenger came, summoning me at once to General Stuart's headquarters, half a mile in front.

Mounting, I rode at a gallop. That was the only gait which Stuart tolerated, except in going *away* from the enemy.

As I rode out of camp I heard "Boots and Saddles" sounded from all the bugles of all the regiments.

I knew then that "something was up." "Boots and Saddles" always meant something when Stuart gave the order.

When I dismounted at headquarters, Stuart himself was waiting, although it was three o'clock in the morning. His plume and golden spurs gleamed through the dark.

"Tell me quick!" was all he had to say. I answered sententiously: "Three rockets went up: red to right, white to left, and blue in the middle."

"You mean *our* right and left, or the enemy's?" he asked eagerly.

"Ours," I answered.

He turned quickly and gave hurried orders to staff-officers, orderlies, and couriers. Then turning to me, he said: "*You ride with me.*" I appreciated the attention.

Five minutes later a great column of cavalrymen were riding at a gallop towards the front. And just as daylight dawned we broke into a charge upon a heavy force of the enemy.

The hostile force was slowly advancing, not expecting us, and we struck it in flank, taking it completely by surprise.

The demoralization of the Manassas, or Bull Run panic had not even yet gone out of the Northern troops. We made short work of their advance and sent them quickly into disorderly retreat.

One of Stuart's couriers was killed in the charge. I remember, because he rode beside me, and his head fell clean from his body, and the sight sickened me, so that I fought harder for the minute than I thought I could.

As the enemy broke, Stuart stopped his horse, slapped his thigh, and turning to me laughing, and with that indifference to rank which always characterized him under excitement, exclaimed: "They haven't got over it yet, have they?"

The Manassas panic always did impress Stuart as an irresistible joke.

A moment later he said: "I'm glad you reported those rockets. Always report whatever you see. Even a shooting star may mean something at headquarters."

But I have never ceased to wonder why we guards that night had no orders to look out for red, white, and blue rockets, since they meant so much. If they had not been reported by a tired and lonely sentinel, we should have been run over in our tents by a force of ten thousand men.

A celebrated writer says: "War is a hazard of possibilities, probabilities, luck, and ill luck."

It was luck that night that a sentry was tired of singing "Juanita" under his breath.

SCRUGGS

SCRUGGS lived throughout the war in that debatable land between the lines in Northern Virginia, where it was always a wonder that anybody could live at all.

And Scruggs lived well, too. He was not able to work, because in order to keep out of the army he had found or feigned a physical disability of some kind.

We always knew that we could get accurate information concerning the enemy by going to Scruggs for it. He frequented their camps as freely as he did ours. He kept his eyes open. He always knew all the important facts, and he was always eager to tell them.

When we went after this information Scruggs was sure to be nowhere visible, and none of his family could ever tell where he might be. But after he had had opportunity to find out with certainty to which side we belonged, Scruggs would come out of his hiding-place, and tell us precisely at what points the enemy was encamped, what his strength was, and what his disposition to activity appeared to be.

Then he would tell us how nearly his family were starving by reason of the fact that the enemy had raided his place and carried off all his supplies. In common gratitude we could do nothing less than replenish his larder with whatever we might happen to possess.

Scruggs's information was always accurate, always full, and always scrupulously truthful.

When a party of the enemy went up to Scruggs's to inquire about us, Scruggs pursued precisely the same policy. First making sure to which side the party belonged, he would come forth and tell all that he knew with regard to the position and strength of our posts; he would add that little piece of misinformation,—most precious to him,—that we had stripped him bare of sustenance, and they would generously relieve his necessities again.

In all this Scruggs was scrupulously truthful, except for the little lie about provisions, and it was all absolutely impartial. If such virtues count for anything in war, Scruggs was entitled to full credit for them.

But one day our commander grew suspicious of Scruggs. On the same day the commander of the Federal outposts began also to suspect Scruggs.

After a little investigation our commandant made up his mind to hang Scruggs for a spy. About the same time the Federal commandant, after a like investigation, came to a similar determination with regard to Scruggs.

The two hanging parties met at Scruggs's house. As usual, Scruggs was not there. But the two parties engaged each other at once. They were about of equal numbers, and they fought valiantly for a time, neither understanding, of course, that they were there on precisely similar errands.

After a little our party began to doubt whether Scruggs was worth the contest or not, and retired a little way. The Federals, with a like contempt for Scruggs, retired about the same distance. After a few shots at long range both parties went back to their camps, each commander feeling that, "After all, Scruggs has never failed to give us all the information he could, and has never yet deceived us on a single point."

After both parties had gone Scruggs came out of his hiding-place and remarked to his eldest daughter: "You see, Prudence, what it is for a feller to be always truthful."

And, by the way, Scruggs never did get himself hanged.

JOE ON HORSEBACK

JOE was not quite seventeen years old.
He could ride anything that happened to possess a back. He therefore had a great love for his horse — the noblest one in the battery.

During the preliminary skirmish in advance of Pocotaligo, on that terrible 22d of October, 1862, his gun detachment was cut to pieces in a fearful way, until he had to work his piece with three men, serving as a cannoneer himself. When we retired from the skirmish line at Yemassee to Pocotaligo proper, and it was obvious that we must fight enormous odds in order to prevent the enemy from crossing the causeway we were defending, I suggested to Joe that he dismount, as the rest of us had done, and take to a tree.

Joe resented the suggestion with the remark: " My place is on horseback. I'm a sergeant."

Two minutes later a cannon-ball carried away his horse's tail. Five seconds afterwards another cannon-ball carried off the beast's left forefoot. Feeling that the horse was sinking under him, Joe dismounted to see what the damage had been. As he stooped to look at the dismembered foot, still another cannon-ball passed just over his head, split his saddle, and broke the poor animal's back. Thereupon Joe turned, presented his pistol at the horse's head, averted his eyes and fired.

Then he took a horse out of the battery and mounted him, remarking: "I still contend that as a sergeant my place is on horseback."

The boy was crying, but none of us made remark upon the incongruity.

Joe was mentioned in general orders for his gallantry that day, but the fact had no reference to this matter of the horse.

A GOOD-BYE TO A FRIEND.

A RATHER BAD NIGHT

WE were living in the deserted village. That is to say, our battery of light artillery was stationed at Bluffton, South Carolina.

At ordinary times Bluffton had a population of about three thousand souls. At the time of which I write it had no population at all.

It was a town built upon a high bluff overlooking an arm of the sea, or more properly a great bay, broken by multitudinous islands into various inlets. Hilton Head lay within sight, twelve miles away, and all the waters of the great island-studded bay were navigable.

Bluffton never had any business to do. It had no shops, no factories, no anything but planters' residences. Its houses were all elegant and all comfortable. Its streets were shaded by great spreading trees, not planted in symmetrical rows, but growing wherever they pleased, in the midst of the thoroughfares.

Bluffton was exposed to the direct assault of gun-boats or expeditions of any sort. So, early in the war, its entire population left and went to points in the interior. At the time I write of, in 1863, there was not a soul in the town except the men of the battery to which I belonged.

Our captain was commandant of outposts. I was adjutant of the same.

Our support consisted of two or three small troops of cavalry. Their camps were several miles in rear of our own. These cavalrymen did all the picketing. In the event of an attack we and they were charged with the duty of harassing the advance of the enemy and delaying him on his march to the railroad, seventeen miles away, long enough for troops to be sent down from Charleston or up from Savannah.

It was a wild, free, gypsy-like life. We lived in the handsomely furnished houses, made free use of the very rich libraries, fished, played at chess, shot deer and turkeys in the woods, dozed upon "joggling boards" in sea-breeze-swept piazzas, and altogether did nothing most industriously and delightfully.

There was one duty to be done, and that a very important one. It was necessary for some officer to make the grand rounds of the pickets every night. This task devolved upon me about once a week. The pickets were stationed at all available points of observation below, all points from which the channels could be seen. To visit them required an all night's ride, which in that country is by no means an agreeable undertaking.

A Rather Bad Night

The weeds rise above the head of a horseman, and the dew drips as rain might, from every leaf. The night rider becomes water soaked and chilled to the very bones, even during the fierce summer weather. During the autumn and winter a night ride on this subtropical coast brings with it a degree of suffering from cold which the fiercest Northern winter never produces.

But it was absolutely necessary to visit the picket posts. Upon their efficiency depended our safety and that of the railroad we were set to defend. If a single picket slept, a fleet of gunboats or ship's launches might come to Bluffton wholly unannounced. The battery, without support at hand, would fall helpless into the enemy's hands, and the railroad communication, on which the safety of Charleston and Savannah depended, would be broken.

It was Christmas Eve, crisp and cool. A heap of fat hard pine was blazing in the great fireplace in our quarters. The negro servant was busy in the kitchen without. Our guests, half a dozen officers from the cavalry companies, were already assembled. We had invited them to dine with us upon a haunch of venison, a wild turkey, fish, oysters, crabs, shrimps, etc., all of which, except the first two, could be taken at any time within a hundred yards of the door. Our little party-giving promised to be a thoroughly successful bit of hospitality.

Curry, the cook, had just begun to put the dinner on the table when a messenger came to report that Lieutenant C——, the officer appointed to make the picket rounds that night, was ill and could not go. It was my turn next and there was no escape. At the holiday season pickets especially need watching. I knew very well it would never do to leave them unvisited that night. There was nothing for it, therefore, but to turn the guests over to my messmate, the captain, and order my horse.

My guide — for without a guide no one could possibly find his way at night through parts of that country — was a dull, taciturn fellow, with whom I found it impossible to maintain a conversation. My twelve miles' ride to the farthest picket post, which I visited first, was therefore a very disagreeable substitute for the jovial, social evening I had planned.

By the time I had reached Bear's Island, I was wet to the skin with dew and stiff with cold. It was about ten o'clock when we rode across the causeway from the mainland to the island, and the first thing I observed was the utter darkness of the place. Ordinarily the pickets on this post kept up a little fire behind a screen at which to warm and dry themselves during the night. Approaching from the rear, I always saw this fire when I crossed the causeway, the screen standing between it and the water on the other side. To-night, however, everything was dark, and it was with some little difficulty that we found our way across the island to the picket post.

"What's the matter, sergeant?" I asked. "Where's your fire to-night?"

"I had to put it out and move away from it," he replied. "They are loading up two gun-boats and three transports just across the creek there, and they threw two or three charges of grape-shot over here an hour or two ago. They killed one of my men, poor fellow. I've been watching them and was on the point of sending a man up with the alarm. I'm glad you've come to take the responsibility off my shoulders."

By this time I had brought my glass to bear upon the pier upon the other side of the inlet, or creek, as it is commonly called, and saw that the sergeant was right. Three transports were rapidly receiving troops, cavalry, artillery, and infantry, while two rather formidable looking gun-boats were sullenly steaming up and down in front.

The inlet was nearly a mile wide, and as the enemy showed few lights and dim ones, the sergeant without a glass had not been able to discover the number of troops taken on board. I soon made out that at least five field batteries had been shipped, and that the transports were almost full of troops, while a battalion of infantry, a squadron of cavalry, and two batteries remained on shore, apparently waiting for those on board to be so disposed as to afford room for them.

I rapidly weighed all the probabilities in my mind. There were two and only two possible purposes in this embarkation of troops. It was a formidable expedition against the railroad, via Bluffton, or else it was merely a removal of troops from one point on the coast to another. If the first were the object, the vessels would steam up the inlet; if the other, they would put to sea.

But if it were merely a transfer of troops, why were the transports crowded in this way, and why were the convoying gun-boats there? There was no enemy off the coast, except storms; and as storms were conspicuously disregarded in the overloading of the steamers, it seemed to me clear that the expedition was bound for Bluffton.

"How many men have you, sergeant?" I asked.

"Two," he replied.

"Trusty fellows?"

"As good as ever threw a leg over a saddle."

"Send them to me," I said.

When they came, I asked: "Are your horses good ones?"

"Pretty good."

A Rather Bad Night   63

"Mount, then," I said to one, "and ride as fast as you can to Buckingham Ferry. Wait with the pickets there till the fleet comes within sight. Then send a man to Bluffton to announce the fact. Stay yourself till the fleet has passed, observing which creek it takes. As soon as you satisfy yourself on that point, ride to Bluffton and report."

Then turning to the other, I said: "You go to Hunting Island and do the same thing. Tell the sergeants there to follow their standing orders in all other regards. Be quick, now, both of you. I'll expect you at Bluffton at the right time."

As the men galloped away, I walked to the place where the sergeant was still standing, and said: "Sergeant, you and I will stay here till the fleet leaves. Then we'll ride straight to Bluffton on a full run and give the alarm in time."

"It's already leaving," he replied. "And look! it's steaming straight up the creek."

Looking, I saw that it was as he said. The two gun-boats abreast led the column, the three transports following.

"It's time for us to be riding, then," I said, hastily springing into my saddle. "But we can beat them by two hours, as the creek is crooked and they must sound all the way for want of buoys."

We galloped across the island; but when we came to the little creek we found an unexpected obstacle in our way. The tide had risen well-nigh to the flood, and was exceedingly high in consequence of a strong wind that had been blowing on shore all day. The strip of marsh which separated the island from the mainland was completely covered with water, and even the causeway leading across it was submerged. The two men sent to alarm the pickets had reached the place only a little while earlier than we. We found them hunting for some landmark or other by which to find out where the causeway lay.

The sergeant thought he knew its locality and direction. He boldly plunged in. The rest of us followed.

Just what we did, or where we went, or how it all happened, none of us ever knew. But we rode off the submerged track, about midway the stream, and found ourselves floundering in the water, some of us on our horses, and some of us under them. It was the darkest night I ever knew. Once in the water we could see no shore anywhere. Naturally, each took the direction in which he thought the desired bank lay. And it seemed that no two of us agreed in our views on this point except by accident.

My horse swam pretty well and finally made the edge of the water. But the bottom was a quagmire, and sinking in it he could not extricate himself. To relieve him I slipped off his back and into the water, but it proved too late. With every frantic struggle the poor beast sank deeper, and within a minute he lay lifeless in the water, half buried in the mud of the bottom.

My own situation was a perilous one. My feet sank at once in the slimy ooze. To save myself I threw my body forwards. Succeeding in freeing my feet, I swam until the water was too shallow for swimming. After that, by crawling on my belly, I managed to avoid sinking and smothering in the mud.

It was half an hour, however, before I stood upon firm ground again, and then I did not know which side of the marsh I had reached.

I was covered with slime, stiff with cold, and utterly exhausted by my exertions. Of myself, however, I thought little. I was anxious only about the sleeping battery at Bluffton. If the alarm were not given, — and unless some one or other of our party had succeeded in getting across with his horse, it could not be, — Bluffton would be taken completely by surprise. The battery would be captured. A rapid march would take the enemy to the railroad, either at Grahamville or at Hardeeville, before any force could be sent to oppose. Our defence of an essential line of communication would fail. Even if the two men from the picket post had got out on the other side, they would go not to Bluffton, but to Buckingham Ferry and Hunting Island, as I had ordered. It was not at all certain that the fleet would pass either of those points. It could sail up other creeks quite as easily, particularly on such a tide as that.

With these thoughts in my mind I felt the need of bestirring myself. I was not long in discovering that we were still on the island, and not on the mainland. Following the margin of the water, I presently came to the two men who had been with the sergeant on picket. One of them was stuck in the mud, and the other was trying to draw him out with a pole. Both of them had lost their horses. The sergeant and my guide had escaped with their steeds, and I found both of them on the island, a little further up the shore.

The guide was utterly demoralized with fright, or cold, or both. So I took his horse and ordered him to wait on the island till morning, and then to make his way to whatever point he should find it easiest to reach. The sergeant and I determined to make another effort to get to Bluffton and give the alarm.

"Run back to the other side of the island," said he to one of his men, "and see if the fleet is still in sight and what it is doing. We must let our horses blow a little, and you can get back by the time we are ready to start."

The man went, and his comrade, having nothing better to do, went with him. Presently one of them returned, bringing the news that the fleet was making its way up a narrow creek from which, as we knew, neither the Buckingham Ferry nor the Hunting Island picket could see it. As those were the only posts from which after seeing it a man could get to Bluffton in time to give the alarm, the sergeant and I were more than ever determined to make our way thither at all hazards. Luckily the road from Bear's Island to Bluffton was the easiest one in all that country to find, and the one I happened to know best. So that even if the sergeant should not get across the marsh, I was confident of my ability to make the journey alone.

"Now," said the sergeant, "if I get across I won't wait for you, but will go right on; if you succeed, don't wait for me. It's no time for ceremony. It's better one of us should drown than that the other should be delayed."

"Spoken like a man and a soldier, sergeant," said I. "Now for it." And with that we again essayed to follow the submerged track. About midway the sergeant's horse went down as before; and just as I was about to call out something encouraging to him the guide's horse, which I was riding, plunged headforemost into the salt water, throwing me completely over his head.

For a moment I was senseless from a blow received either from the hoof of the sergeant's horse, or by falling against one of the timbers of the causeway. When I came to myself I was clinging to the tail of the sergeant's horse, while the sergeant, as I presently discovered, was holding by one of the stirrups.

How long we remained in the water, I do not know, but it must have been nearly an hour. The poor horse swam around in a purposeless way, not knowing where to go, until finally he sank exhausted beneath the tide. Cool as the night was the salt water was tepid as it always is on that coast. Otherwise I should not now be alive to tell of that Christmas Eve.

We got out at last and found ourselves on the island again. Despairing now — for without horses it was simply impossible to get to Bluffton until long after the time when our coming would be of any use — we trudged doggedly across the island, that we might wait and listen at the water's edge for the booming of the cannon.

Two more utterly wretched young men no Christmas morning ever dawned upon.

"See there," said the sergeant, halting suddenly. "There's the fleet, and bless my soul it's putting to sea."

It was true enough. No attack was to be made after all. We had spent the night drowning horses, and nearly drowning ourselves for nothing.

Why the fleet had steamed several miles up the creek before putting to sea, I have never been able to guess. But I vividly remember that its prank subjected me to a twelve miles' walk that morning, and compelled me to substitute quinine and dogwood-root-bark bitters that day for the Christmas dinner I had planned.

THE WOMEN OF PETERSBURG

WE went into Petersburg in June, 1864, with the horses at a brisk trot, and the men on foot at a double quick.

The enemy's battalions were already at the other end of Sycamore Street, and it was our task to drive them back before they should be reinforced.

Nevertheless those good women of Petersburg ministered to us. They knew that we had been marching all night and that we were in a famishing condition. They knew also that we must not waste a moment if Petersburg, the key to Richmond, was not to be lost.

So they formed themselves in platoons — God bless them! — bearing gifts of sandwiches and coffee.

We could not stop even to take, much less to eat, the food they offered, so they thrust their platoons between ours and marched backward as fast as we marched forward, serving their food and drink to us as we went.

Every now and then a Federal shell would come bowling down the street, but these alert women would jump it as nimbly as if its passage had been a prearranged figure in the dance. Not one of them showed the slightest fear. Not one of them faltered for a moment in her ministrations in consideration of herself. There was not one of them, I think, who would not have gone with us into the crash of the battle itself; but by the time we had refreshed ourselves a little, we were so near to the aggressive enemy's lines, that we cried aloud with one voice the order for the womenkind to go back.

A minute later we were in the thick of the struggle for Petersburg. The enemy was not in such force as we had supposed, and we had fortunately arrived some hours in advance of General Grant's ponderous divisions. After fifteen minutes of hard fighting the enemy retired beyond the Jerusalem turnpike and we spent the night in beginning that thin line of earthworks which was destined for eight months to come to hold at bay a force two or three times as strong in numbers as our own.

At any hour during all that eight months the Federal forces could have broken through our lines at any point they pleased, if they had been resolute.

Anybody who will look at the old works today, as I have recently done, and consider the facts dispassionately, can see this clearly for himself. Our enemies had behind them, and running parallel with their lines, a system of roads that was out of our sight. They had resources practically illimitable. They had in front of them an attenuated line of men, stretched out for twenty miles, and without the possibility of reinforcement from any source. They could have concentrated any force they pleased at any point they pleased and at any time they pleased, without the possibility of our discovering what they were doing. They could have made an irresistible attack upon any point of our line at will. They did not do it. And so the fight went on.

During all those weary months the good women of Petersburg went about their household affairs with fifteen-inch shells dropping occasionally into their boudoirs or uncomfortably near to their kitchen ranges. Yet they paid no attention to any danger that threatened themselves.

Their deeds of mercy will never be adequately recorded until the angels report. But this much I want to say of them — they were "war women" of the most daring and devoted type. When there was need of their ministrations on the line, they were sure to be promptly there; and once, as I have recorded elsewhere in print, a bevy of them came out to the lines only to encourage us, and, under a fearful fire, sang Bayard Taylor's "Song of the Camp," giving us as an encore the lines: —

> "Ah, soldiers, to your honored rest,
> Your truth and valor bearing,
> The bravest are the tenderest,
> The loving are the daring."

With inspiration such as these women gave us, it was no wonder that, as I heard General Sherman say soon after the war: "It took us four years, with all our enormous superiority in resources, to overcome the stubborn resistance of those men."

HAM SEAY

HAM SEAY had a hæmorrhage that morning — a hæmorrhage from the lungs.

But Ham Seay had the fastest horse in the company, and he knew how to ride a horse for all that was in him of achievement.

When the news came that Stuart wanted to communicate as quickly as possible with the commandant at Fredericksburg, Ham Seay volunteered to carry the message.

"But you're ill," said Stuart.

"That doesn't matter," said Ham. "I can ride my horse, and my horse is a good one."

"But you're ill," said Stuart again. "And I don't want to send an ill man on such a journey as this."

Then Ham Seay rose in the majesty of his manhood.

"General," he said, "I am a doomed man. I cannot live long to render service in the war. I want to render what service I can. I want to carry this message. It will do me no harm. It will not shorten the few days I have yet to live. It will make my life worth something."

So Stuart gave him the message to a general fifty miles away.

Ham Seay mounted, and said to his comrades: "Good-by, boys. I may never see you again; but I'll do this errand all right, or die trying."

He rode his horse with urgency, but with discretion. He had but one object in view, and that was to get the message to its destination in the briefest possible number of hours.

He delivered his communication. He died half an hour afterwards. His horse had died before Ham did. But both had done their duty.

OLD JONES'S DASH

OLD Jones was a queer character. He was also a queer figure. He never had a uniform. He wore a yellow coat and a pair of light blue trousers. He wore a pot hat of the fashion, I should say at a guess, of the year 1812.

He was a graduate of West Point, but he had resigned from the army twelve years before the war began, and therefore was not entitled to what they called "relative rank."

He was a cynic and a misanthrope. He was still more pronouncedly a misogynist. He did not believe in men. He positively disbelieved in women. He was ready at any time to affront a man and to treat a woman with conspicuous contempt. He hated life, and was ready to give it up at any moment which might suit the decrees or the aspirations of Fate. He was ready to fight anything in the world, or anybody, under any circumstances, or upon any issue.

That is why he got himself cashiered toward the end of the war.

But we are dealing with the beginning of the

war. At the beginning of the war he organized a company of cavalry and got himself elected its captain. In the regular order of promotion he soon came to be colonel of the regiment. It was at this time that the events recorded in the present story occurred.

When McClellan took command of the Army of the Potomac, after the stampede at Manassas, it was under the demoralization of the fearful panic. It was a part of McClellan's program to send his men out on expeditions of attack in order to accustom them to the idea of standing fire. As the end of the summer of 1861 drew near, he had begun, seriously, to threaten our position at Centreville.

He would send out men in considerable force and compel us to meet them with serious intent. Usually Stuart was able very quickly to discover the sham character of these advances. But once in a while they were so well disguised as to be mistaken for serious attacks.

One day in the autumn the greatest of all these advances began. The enemy came forward with every possible appearance of intending an assault on the Confederate position at Centreville.

There were cavalry, infantry, and artillery in the column; and when they reached our picket lines there was every appearance of serious conflict in prospect,

As we sat there on our horses in front of the line, Stuart came along and said to Colonel Jones: "Colonel, I wish you'd take a dozen or twenty men, get into the rear of that force, and find out how much it means."

Jones detailed the requisite number of us from the right of our company, with Captain Irving in command of them. By riding three or four miles to the right, we were able to get in rear of the Federal force. We soon found that there was no baggage train, no commissary train, no quartermaster's train, and no ammunition train — in short, that the advance was not intended as a serious attack.

By the time that we had found out all this, we were within fifty yards of the rear of the Federal lines, and almost immediately opposite the point where we had left our own command. We were pretty well hidden by the underbrush of the woods, as we stood there and looked.

Presently old Jones turned to Charlie Irving and said: "The whole thing's an egg-shell, isn't it?"

"Yes," said Charlie; "an egg-shell easily crushed."

Jones thought a moment, and then said, with his nasal drawl: "I wish I could communicate with Stuart. I'd break through that line and save the trouble of the ride around."

The young captain's eyes snapped with that

peculiar sense of humor and that daring which were his principal characteristics, as he said: "Why not break through anyhow, colonel? Don't you think Stuart would understand? I've never found him slow in getting to windward of things."

"Well, if you say so, captain, I guess we'll do it. It'll save the horses, anyhow. Attention, men!" with a slow drawl. "Draw — sabres! Forward — march! Trot — march! Gallop — march! CHARGE!"

We went through that egg-shell with an enthusiasm which was *not* a reflection of the drawling commands of our colonel.

Captain Irving was right: Stuart was not slow in getting to windward of things. He ordered a charge and doubled up that column like a telescope.

A WOMAN'S HAIR

AFTER the battle of Manassas or Bull Run, fought July 21, 1861, Stuart made his headquarters in the neighborhood of Fairfax Court House, with pickets at Falls Church, Vienna, and other points ten miles or so to the front.

Suddenly, with a strong force, he occupied Mason's and Munson's hills, almost under the guns of the Washington fortifications, and very much farther in advance than outposts generally are.

It has since been a puzzle to many military critics to guess why he did this unusual thing. Perhaps this story may throw some light on the problem.

Our company was on picket at Falls Church. Half a dozen of us kept watch at the edge of the woods on the top of the hill, while the rest of the boys took their ease in rear.

It was in that early stage of the war when to shoot at men seemed to many civilians a species of sport — a sort of pursuit of big game.

This Falls Church post was a favorite rendezvous for this species of sportsmen from Washington. Our position was an exposed one. Men not in the army, and even women, liked to ride out from Washington, crouch behind a pile of logs, and "take a crack" at the rebels.

Now and then they made a widow and some orphans, and since this was merely a matter of diversion and entertainment for them, with no other principle involved, it seemed almost too bad.

Finally Charlie Irving got "tired," as he put it, of "playing partridge for those people to shoot at." Charlie Irving was our captain. He was a man who never said much, but always meant a good deal.

The next morning he made the detail for post duty at the front upon a new principle. We had been nine days on picket, and it had been his custom to detail the men for post duty in front in alphabetical order. This morning he selected us without reference to our "turns," and with sole reference to the speed and endurance of our horses.

"Now, boys," he said, with that easy familiarity which made us call him "Charlie," because we had all gone hunting together as comrades before the war; "now, boys, we're going to capture that picket post to-day, and if I find a civilian among them, I'm going to hang him to that chestnut tree for murder."

We knew that he would do what he said, and

we were all in hearty sympathy with his purpose.

About ten o'clock in the morning the sharpshooting began. Our captain instantly divided us into two squads, and without military formalities said: "Now, boys, ride to the right and left and corner 'em."

That was the only command we received, but we obeyed it with a will. The two sharp-shooting citizens who were there that morning escaped on good horses, but we captured the pickets.

Among them was a woman — a Juno in appearance, with a wealth of raven black hair twisted carelessly into a loose knot under the jockey cap she wore.

She was mounted on a superb chestnut mare, and she knew how to ride.

She might easily have escaped, and at one time seemed about to do so, but at the critical moment she seemed to lose her head and so fell into our hands.

When we brought her to Charlie Irving she was all smiles and graciousness, and Charlie was all blushes.

"You'd hang me to a tree, if I were a man, I suppose," she said. "And serve me right, too. As I'm only a woman, you'd better send me to General Stuart, instead."

This seemed so obviously the right way out

of it that Charlie ordered Ham Seay and me to escort her to Stuart's headquarters, which were under a tree some miles in the rear.

When we got there Stuart seemed to recognize the young woman. Or perhaps it was only his habitual and constitutional gallantry that made him come forward with every manifestation of welcome, and himself help her off her horse, taking her by the waist for that purpose.

Ham Seay and I being mere privates were ordered to another tree. But we could not help seeing that cordial relations were quickly established between our commander and this young woman. We saw her presently take down her magnificent back hair and remove from it some papers. They were not "curl papers," or that sort of stuffing which women call "rats." Stuart was a very gallant man, and he received the papers with much fervor. He spread them out carefully on the ground, and seemed to be reading what was written or drawn upon them.

Then he talked long and earnestly with the young woman and seemed to be coming to some definite sort of understanding with her.

Then she dined with him on some fried salt pork and some hopelessly indigestible fried paste which we called bread.

Then he mounted her on her mare again and summoned Ham Seay and me.

"Escort this young lady back to Captain Irving," he said. "Tell him to send her to the Federal lines under flag of truce, with the message that she was inadvertently captured in a picket charge, and that as General Stuart does not make war on women or children, he begs to return her to her home and friends."

We did all this.

The next day, Stuart with a strong force advanced to Mason's and Munson's hills.

From there we could clearly see a certain house in Washington. It had many windows, and each had a dark Holland shade.

When we stood guard we were ordered to observe minutely and report accurately the slidings up and down of those Holland shades.

We never knew what three shades up, two half up, and five down might signify. But we had to report it, nevertheless, and Stuart seemed from that time to have an almost preternatural advance perception of the enemy's movements.

That young woman certainly had a superb shock of hair.

A MIDNIGHT CRIME

THE CRIMINAL'S OWN ACCOUNT OF IT

AS there is no law that can now reach my crime, I may as well tell all about it.

Soon after we sat down before Petersburg, in the summer of 1864, I was sent on a little military mission accompanied by Johnny Garrett, into the land of desolation — that part of Northern Virginia which lay sometimes in the possession of one army, sometimes in possession of the other, but was mostly left in nobody's possession at all, and open to raids from both sides.

That region had been swept by fire and sword for nearly four years. It had been tramped over by both armies, and latterly had been subjected to that process of destruction which Sheridan had in mind when he said of another region that "the crow that flies over it must carry his rations with him."

How anybody managed to live at all in such a region has always been a puzzle, but a few people did.

We had slept, Johnny Garrett and I, by the side of a fence the night before, and without breakfast we had been riding all day. Late in the afternoon we made up our minds to go for supper and lodging to a great country house which I had frequently visited as a guest in the days of its abundance. As we rode through the plantation, decay manifested itself on every hand. There was a small, straggling crop in process of growth, but sadly ill attended. There were no animals in sight except five sheep that we saw grazing on a hillside.

As we turned the corner of the woodland the mansion came into view. Only its walls were left standing. Fire had destroyed the rest. At the gate we met an old negro serving-man, whom I had known in the palmy days as Uncle Isham.

When I had seen him last he was in livery. As I saw him *now* he was in rags.

Some eager, hurried inquiries as to the family brought out the fact that the mistress of the mansion with her two grown daughters was living in one of the negro quarters in rear of the burned house, and that he, alone, remained as a servant on the plantation.

" Dey took all de res' off No'th, an' dey tried to take Isham, too. But Isham he slip' de bridle one night, an' he came back heah to look after ole missus an' de girls. So heah I is, an' heah Ise gwine to stay."

We did not remain to hear Isham's account

of his adventures, but hurried on to find out the condition of things with the family. There were but two rooms — one below, and the other above stairs — in the hut in which they were living. Yet the proud woman who was thus reduced showed no shame of her poverty, but gloried in it rather, as the old soldier glories in the scars received in his country's service.

She welcomed us with as warm a show of hospitality as she had ever made in the old days of lavish entertainment.

After our first inquiries concerning their welfare, she said to us laughingly: "I wouldn't keep you to-night, but would send you on to a better place, if I knew any better in the neighborhood. As it is, you'll have to sleep under the trees for lack of room; but you boys are rather used to that. As for supper, I can give you some corn-bread and some sorghum molasses. The bread won't be very good, because our supply of salt has run out, and of course as the cows have all been killed I can't give you butter. But there's enough bread and sorghum, anyhow."

"How long since you had meat?" I asked.

"About three weeks," she replied. "That is to say, since the last big raiding party came by."

"Have you no pigs left?"

"No, we haven't a living animal of any kind."

"Whose sheep are those I saw as I rode up?"

"They belong to a neighbor," she answered. "They're what's left of a large flock. When the raiders were here those five sheep ran into the bushes and escaped. But even if they were ours, you know, we couldn't kill one."

I remembered then that a law of the Confederacy made it a crime severely punishable to slaughter a sheep, even one's own. They were wanted by the government for their wool to clothe the army.

Waiving all this aside as a matter of small moment, our hostess pressed us again to dismount for supper.

At this point Johnny Garrett lied:

"Oh, we can't stay to supper, and the fact is we couldn't eat if we did. It's only half an hour since we ate the best part of a ham out of our haversacks. And besides we've got to get to Gordonsville to-night."

I am afraid I was accessory after the fact to the telling of that lie. At least I didn't contradict it.

We pushed on a little way till we had got out of sight of the house. Then we stopped by mutual consent under a tree and dismounted.

"The grass is pretty good," I said, "and we'll let the horses crop it while we wait for it to get good and dark." It did not seem necessary to mention what we were to wait for darkness for.

"Yes," said Johnny, "there are the sheep, and I'll keep an eye on them."

When it was thoroughly dark we committed a double crime.

It was sheep stealing as well as a violation of the other law, but we were not in a mood to consider such things just then. Under cover of the darkness we killed the fattest sheep in the lot, dressed it as well as we could, and then by the light of some matches I wrote a little note on a leaf from my memorandum book. It said simply this: —

"There is no law to forbid some hungry women to eat a sheep that somebody else has killed in violation of law."

Pinning this to the carcass we carried the mutton to the house, and hung it to a tree where it would be seen with the dawn.

We felt as well about this thing as if we had been engaged in some highly moral act.

A LITTLE REBEL

IT was an odd kind of a situation. It was in 1862, and we were on the coast of South Carolina defending the railroad line between Charleston and Savannah.

We had no infantry supports, and artillery is supposed to be helpless without such supports. But as there was nothing on the other side, except those pestilent sharp-shooters in the Hayward mansion, we did not need support.

It was our business to shell that mansion, burn it, and drive the sharp-shooters out. I may say, parenthetically, that we didn't like the business. Mr. Hayward, who was familiarly known as "Tiger Bill," had been the friend of our battery ever since we had succeeded in putting out a fire that had burnt some thousands of panels of fence for him. It is true that his friendship for us was in the main a reflex of his enmity to the Charleston Light Dragoons and the Routledge Mounted Riflemen. He favored us mainly to spite them. Nevertheless he favored us. He sent a wagon every morning to our camp loaded with vegetables, fruits, suck-

She was singing "Dixie."

ling pigs, and whatever else his dozen plantations might afford.

Naturally, we did not like the job of burning one of his country houses. But as business is business, so in war orders are orders.

Half a dozen shells did the work. Flames burst from the house in every direction, and the enemy's sharp-shooters who had been using it as a vantage ground rapidly retreated across the cotton fields to the woodlands beyond under fire of our guns.

Our captain, a great bearded warrior, six feet four inches high, and as rough as men are made in appearance, was suddenly seized with a tender thought. Turning to me, he said: "There may be some poor devil wounded in that house and likely to be roasted. Let's ride over there and see."

We put spurs to our horses, dashed through the sharp-shooters' fire, and a few minutes later began exploring the lower quarters of the house, the fire being above. We found nothing till we came to the cellar. There we discovered a little girl, anywhere from two to three years old,— I'm not a good judge of little girls' ages,— sitting in a little rocking-chair, and singing "Dixie."

The captain grabbed her suddenly and ran to the open air with her, for the volumes of smoke were rapidly penetrating to the cellar. When he got her out, he said: "Who are you?"

She replied, in a piping little voice, "I'm *Lulalie*."

Whether this meant that her name was Lula Lee, or Eulalie, or what, we could not make out.

"Where is your mamma?" asked the captain.

"She's dead — she died when I was born."

"Where is your papa?"

"I don't know. Those ugly other people took him away. When he saw 'em coming, he took me to the cellar, and told me to stay there so the shellies wouldn't hit me."

"Where's your maumey?" (Maumey meaning in South Carolina "negro nurse.")

"I don't know," she answered. "Those ugly other people took all the colored folks away."

Just then the battery advanced with its colors flying. Looking up the little girl recognized the Confederate battle banner and said: "That's *my kind of a flag*. I don't like that ugly other striped thing."

Manifestly the child was without protectors. We adopted her in the name of the battery.

When we returned to the camp several serious questions arose. Jack Hawkins, one of the ex-circus clowns of the battery, suggested that first of all we must secure a chaperone for her. When asked what he meant by that, he said with lordly superiority: "Well, you see, chaperone is French for nurse. We want a nurse for this little child."

"Nonsense," said Denton, the other ex-circus clown, "you don't know any more about the proprieties than you do about French. Chaperone means somebody to look after a church, and this little girl isn't even a chapel. We'll look after her, and we don't want no nurse to help."

The captain, with his long beard, was holding the little child in his arms all this time, and she suddenly turned around to him and seizing his beard said: "I like your big whiskers. They are like my papa's. You don't bite, because you've got hair on your face?"

"No, dear," he replied, "I don't bite such as you."

But he was very much given to biting, all the same — as the enemy had more than once found out.

"First of all," said Denton, who was nothing if not practical, "the little girl's got to have some clothes."

Denton was a tailor, as well as a clown, and naturally his thoughts were the first to run in that groove.

"I ain't much used to making girl's clothes, but a tailor's a tailor, and if anybody'll provide me the materials, I'll undertake to fix up some gowns for her."

Tom Booker, who was much given to riding around the country, said at once: "I know where the mortal remains of an old store repose, up at Gillisonville, about nine miles away. If I had any money—"

Every man thrust his hand into his pocket, and each drew out what he had. The sum total was more than adequate. When Tom returned a few hours later there were no "mortal remains" of that store left. He brought back with him thirty-seven yards of highly colored calico, of different patterns, one red blanket, a box full of galloon trimming, something that he called "gimp," two bolts of domestic, three cans of tomatoes, and two bottles of chow-chow, besides a dozen quarter cases of sardines and two kegs of cove oysters.

He dumped the merchandise on the ground with the remark: "There, I've closed that store."

Denton made some invidious remarks reflecting upon Tom's taste in the selection of calicoes, etc., adding the suggestion that there was galloon enough and "gimp" enough in the invoice "to upholster all the women in Charleston for the next six months — if they liked that kind of thing."

Nevertheless, he set to work with a will. Within a day or two the little lady was provided with gowns and night-gowns, and underclothes sufficient in quantity, at least, though perhaps not made strictly in accordance with the latest fashions in gear of that kind. Indeed, Denton had succeeded in making her look very much hindsidebefore. The little girl's gowns all buttoned down in front. But the little girl was pleased with what she called the "gownies" and sometimes the "pritties." Their barbaric colors tickled her taste so much that Denton decided to make her a cloak out of the flaming red blanket.

When it was put on her, her glory was complete. She said: "It looks like my kind of a flag," referring to the red of the battle banner.

* * * * *

She was taken away from us presently by a committee of good women of the neighborhood. She became the protégée of a lady whose whole life had been given to caring for other people, including our battery.

Denton, however, put in a claim to the privilege of continuing to fashion her clothes.

"You see I've got the whole stock of that store on my hands; and since I learned dressmaking, I've a fancy to perfect myself. And you see I've got fond of the little girl."

A couple of tears trickled down the hoary old sinner's cheek, and Mrs. Hutson consented.

Every day after roll-call the captain sent a delegation to the Hutsons' house to ask after the battery's child. Every day when we drilled at the guns the little girl herself came in her barbaric costume to see what she called her "shooties," meaning the cannoneers.

We had to part with our little girl presently, we being under orders, and she stationed. As we moved away from the station on our flat cars, she stood upon the platform, and waved "her kind of a flag" at us, crying, throwing kisses, and calling out: "Good-by, you good shooties."

I think the morals of the battery were distinctly better after this little episode.

TWENTY-ONE

AFTER the battle of Bull Run, or Manassas, as we called it, the region north of Fairfax Court House was a No-man's land.

Little by little we occupied it during that summer, even to Mason's and Munson's hills. But the process of occupation was slow. When we pressed forward immediately after the battle all that region was *terra incognita*.

About half the people inhabiting it were loyal to one side; about half to the other. So in asking information we had to be circumspect.

But we had assurance that the Hopes were loyal to our side. So when Lieutenant Billy Wilds was sent out with a party of us, on scouting duty, he naturally went to the Hope mansion for information.

He got it in abundance. Charlotte Hope, the daughter of the house, came out to give it to us, and she was very enthusiastic. She was a brunette, full of life, full of health, and full of enthusiasm for the cause. Besides, she knew how to sit gracefully on a rail fence. She had a rich contralto voice that had narrowly escaped being a bass. She was beautiful to her finger tips. She "had a way with her" that was fascinating beyond belief.

As she sat there on the rail fence, explaining the geography of the region round about, we all fell in love with her as troopers should, so far at least as to be ready to do any conceivable deed of derring-do in her behalf. But Lieutenant Wilds fell in love with her in fuller fashion, as was afterwards made manifest.

She sat there on the fence curled up most entrancingly and expounded the geography of the country with great minuteness. But when she tried to tell us just where a certain strong Federal post was, which we very much wanted to attack, she grew impatient of words.

Turning to a negro boy she said: "Saddle Saladin. I'll go and show them."

Three minutes later she was in the saddle. Half an hour afterwards Charlie Irving, our captain who had joined us and taken command, gently ordered her to the rear. As I have related in another book of reminiscences she refused to obey. She said: "I believe you are going to charge those fellows, and I want to see the fun."

Well, she saw the fun. We made the charge. At the end of it Lieutenant Wilds was more in love with her than ever.

As we escorted her back to her home she

broke into song. Her song was the old English ballad which begins: —

> "In days of old, when knights were bold,
> And barons held their sway."

As she sang, she laid special stress upon two passages in the ballad. One was the line where the hero says: —

> "I'll live for love or die."

The other was, where as death overcomes him he sings: —

> "I've kept the vow I swore."

The song seemed, whether prophetically or otherwise, to have entered this young girl's soul and to have taken possession of her spirit.

It was not long afterwards that we learned that our gallant young lieutenant was engaged to be married to Charlotte Hope. The marriage was to take place as soon as the war was over. At that time we regarded this as a postponement of only a few months at most. We expected to win then and we expected to win quickly.

Whenever Lieutenant Wilds was sent upon a scouting expedition, he found it imperatively necessary to call at the Hope mansion for geographical and other information, though by this time we had all become familiar with every road and footpath in that quarter of Virginia.

It was a little fiction we were all pleased to love him for. One day about a month later, while we were waiting in the yard for Lieutenant Wilds to secure the necessary geographical information indoors, a Federal force attacked us. The lieutenant came out promptly, swung himself into the saddle, and ordered a charge. We fought there under the cherry trees for full fifteen minutes. At the end of the contest the enemy was driven away, and we pursued — but three of our saddles were empty.

One of them was that of Lieutenant Wilds.

* * * * *

It was Charlotte's wish that Lieutenant Wilds should be buried in the family grave-yard of the Hopes. It was also her wish that his company should attend the funeral.

We brought two other companies along to stand guard and prevent any possible interruption of the ceremonies. We buried our comrade with all military honors. We fired the conventional salute over the grave.

Then we proceeded to attack a military force which had come up, intent upon disturbing the obsequies.

But before we moved off, Charlotte, who had been dry-eyed from the first, came to one of us and said: "He was just twenty-one. It will take just twenty-one to pay for him."

* * * * *

It was only two or three days later when Charlie Hopper rode into the camp on a magnificent chestnut-sorrel mare. We did not know him.

He said he didn't want to enlist. He merely wanted to join the company. He explained that if he enlisted he would be a man under pay. And he didn't want pay, he said, for the work he wanted to do. Only give him rations and a chance and he would be satisfied.

His idea of a chance soon developed itself. He wanted to be as continually as possible in the presence of the enemy, anywhere, anyhow. He wanted to shoot all the "Yankees" he could. For that purpose he had brought with him the first Whitworth rifle I ever saw, with its long range, its telescopic sights, and its terrible accuracy of fire.

He seemed about sixteen years old. He didn't tell us anything about himself, not even where he came from. But he had a long talk, and a confidential one, with Charlie Irving. After that Charlie paid him special attention. He detailed him upon every scouting expedition that had "business" in it. Sometimes when scouting expeditions were slack, the young fellow would go off by himself and remain for a day or two in close proximity to the enemy's lines.

Each day he wore upon his breast a little tag with a number on it.

One day when the number had reached seventeen, he and I lay together behind a sycamore log, shooting at a peculiarly pestilent picket post. After one of his shots he called out, "Eighteen." The next shot was simultaneous, he and I firing together. The man at whom we fired fell forward over his log, evidently dead.

Charlie Hopper turned to me and said: "You fired at the same moment I did; it's a disputed bird. I can't count him."

Full of curiosity I asked: "What do you mean, Hopper?"

He answered: "Nothing — Just counting — Settling a score!"

It was only a few days later when we were at Falls Church. Young Hopper's score read twenty, when he asked permission to ride out and personally encounter an officer who had separated himself from his command. The permission was given. Hopper leaped upon his mare, drew his sword, and galloped toward the officer. They met in mid field. The officer fired just as the boy clove him to the saddle. Hopper fell forward on his horse and rode back to the lines.

As he rolled off the saddle, he said: "I'm done for, boys, but I've made it twenty-one without counting a single disputed bird." Then, feebly, he broke into song, singing, —

"I've kept the vow I swore."

Before we buried him in the *Hope cemetery* the next day, the captain told me that Charlie Hopper was none other than Charlotte Hope.

But I had guessed the secret that day when she had refused to count the "disputed bird."

A BEEF EPISODE

WE had no rations at Bluffton, in South Carolina.

The sea was there with its multitudinous fish, and crabs and shrimps, and with its mountainous banks of oysters. There were turkeys and deer and squirrels in the woods, and quail and marsh fowl in the fields. We were expected to take care of ourselves.

But one cannot shoot turkeys, or deer, or squirrels with a twelve-pounder Napoleon. And as for the sea food, while we rejoiced in it for a time, we became desperately weary of it after a while.

We began, therefore, to frequent Bull Island. Bull Island lay near Hilton Head, which the enemy occupied. Bull Island had been abandoned at the beginning of the war, and the cattle on the plantations there had gone wild, breeding as buffalo might.

Here was a source of supply. We resolved to avail ourselves of it. About twice a week we sent expeditions over there in whale-boats, and killed a bullock or a cow or two, dressed the meat and brought it home, taking care to bring the skin also, in order that our half-crazy doctor might experiment on it with his new process for quick tanning. As an incident, I may remark that not one of us ever got a pair of boots out of those hides.

The enemy on Hilton Head were also more or less in lack of beef. They, too, discovered Bull Island, and frequented it with a purpose similar to our own.

One day Joe went over there with sixteen men in a boat carrying that number of oars, and pretty well rigged for sailing. He had no sooner got his command into the cane-brake in search of cattle, than he discovered a party of Federals immediately in front of him. In the dense growth of the forest he could have no idea whatever of his enemy's strength. His one thought was, to avoid the capture of his force. To that end he must make as brave a show of strength as possible. He therefore ordered his little squad of men to scatter themselves out over a line of three or four hundred yards, and to keep up as continuous a fire as possible.

The enemy's line seemed to be of about equal length, and their fire about the same as his. It was a little before ten o'clock in the morning when this thing began, and it was not until after dusk that the two forces sneaked simultaneously to their boats.

Neither had any beef, and each discovered that the other was numerically about equal to itself.

So far as we were ever able to discover, nobody had been killed or wounded on either side. A day had been wasted in futile firing through the cane. Both sides had been disappointed of their provisions.

Neither had injured the other, neither had gained any benefit, and the cattle had had a good time.

Thirty years afterwards Joe and the sergeant on the other side met, and one said to the other: "After all it would have been better if we had turned our backs on each other that day. There were cattle on both sides." The other answered: "Yes, but that would have been the wise way of peace; we were engaged in the barbarism of war."

BERNARD POLAND'S PROPHECY

I DO not pretend to understand it at all.
The best theories I have ever been able to form, whether physiological or psychological, or a mixture of the two, have utterly failed to account to my mind for the facts in Bernard Poland's case.

I tell the story, therefore, without trying to explain it.

In the year 1857 I became a student in a Virginian college not far from Richmond. When I took possession of my quarters in the building three or four days before the session began, I was an entire stranger to every one there. As I had already spent two years in another college, I knew the importance of using circumspection in the choice of friends in such a place, so that I was in no hurry to make acquaintances. It was my deliberate purpose, indeed, to avoid all intercourse with my fellow-students, until such time as I should discover who and what they were.

But one morning — the next after my arrival, I think it was — as I sat in the great stone portico, two students, evidently old acquaintances, and both of them members of the college during the previous year, stood near me discussing some matter or other, I forget what.

The younger was bantering and teasing the other by expressing all sorts of unconventional, radical, and even revolutionary opinions, which his friend took the trouble seriously to combat, greatly to the younger man's amusement, as I could see. Their conversation did not impress me in the least, except as it revealed to me something in the younger man's mind and character which fascinated me unaccountably.

His age was about the same as mine. His scholarship was about equally advanced, as I learned when we entered the same class. Like myself he had been an omnivorous reader; but where I had read with a disposition to select and criticise and differ, he appeared to have read with the most hospitable mind I ever knew. He gave at least a *quasi*-belief to everything that literature had to offer for his entertainment. He was very slender, even to frailty of body. He had a thin and not handsome face, rather sharp features, lips on which there was a singularly joyous smile, and great gray eyes filled with an extraordinary sadness. The mouth and eyes contradicted each other so flatly, that during all the years of our acquaintance I was never quite able to persuade myself that they properly belonged to the same countenance;

that one or the other portion of the face was not always hiding behind a mask. The effect was indescribable; and among all the men and women I have ever known I have seen nothing else like it.

I knew nothing about the man except as I had caught from conversation that his name was Bernard Poland. Yet the moment I saw him, and listened to his chatter, I made up my mind that he should be my closest friend. I felt that between him and me there would grow up that intellectual sympathy which is the only secure basis of friendship between men.

Not that he and I were at all alike in any way. Indeed, two more utterly unlike personalities it would be difficult to find or imagine. I was serious; he playful, always. I was robust and inclined to plume myself somewhat upon my muscularity; while he was delicate both in frame and health, and cared next to nothing for any of the rougher sports in which I took almost an insane delight. Intellectually, too, we were exact opposites, as I have already hinted. I was inclined to doubt and to question all things, rejecting all that I failed to comprehend and account for; he was something of a mystic — not superstitious, but abounding in faith, and still more in the possibilities of faith.

He was never quite ready, dogmatically, to reject anything, however incapable of proof it might be, so long as it was also incapable of positive and conclusive refutation.

He was not credulous exactly, yet he scouted no superstition which was not either manifestly or demonstrably absurd.

All this I learned afterwards, however. At present I was not even acquainted with him, though I had made up my mind to introduce myself after the free and easy manner that obtains among schoolmates.

When he had finished his bantering talk with his fellow-student, he walked away to his room, which was in sight as I sat there in the portico. The other student strolled down the roadway leading to the great gates. He had no sooner gone than Bernard Poland came out again, and walking up to me said: "You and I ought to be friends, and will be, I think. My name is Bernard Poland. What's yours? This is a singular way to introduce oneself, but I can't help it. The moment I saw you sitting there I made up my mind that you and I would be chums. What do you say, old fellow?"

To say that I was astonished is to express my feelings feebly. I was startled, almost frightened, at his words, which were identically those that I had been revolving in my mind as a possible or impossible introductory address to him.

We were friends at once. And though I have known many other friendships, I have known none closer or more satisfactory than that then formed with Bernard Poland. We became, as he said, "Chums."

During the long vacation Bernard spent many weeks with me at my home, and I in turn visited him in a delightful old Virginian house, where father, mother, brother, and sister held him in tenderest regard as their chief object of affection.

After our college days were done we missed no opportunity of spending a day or a week together, our affection suffering no diminution and knowing no change.

One day in 1859, or about that time, we were riding together over a beautiful region in Northern Virginia. We talked of a hundred things, as was our custom. Among them a number of metaphysical and psychological things came up for discussion.

"Do you know," said Bernard presently, "I sometimes think prophecy isn't so strange a thing after all as most people think it. I really see no reason why any earnest man might not be able to foresee the future now and then in moments of exaltation."

"There's reason enough to my mind," I replied, "in the fact that future events do not exist as yet. We cannot know that which is not, though we may shrewdly guess it at times. But when we do, we are only arguing from known or suspected causes to their necessary consequences. And that is in no proper sense prophecy at all."

"Your argument is good enough, but the premises are bad, I think," replied my friend, meditatively, his mouth wreathed with a smile, but his great sad eyes looking solemnly into mine.

"How so?" I asked.

"Why! I doubt the truth of your assumption that future events do not exist as yet."

"Well, go on; I'm ready to hear your explanation or your theory or whatever else it is," said I, laughingly.

"Oh, I don't know that the idea is mine at all. I suppose that others have gone over the ground before me, though I think, perhaps, my application of the thought is new. What I have in mind is this: Past and Future are only divisions of TIME. They do not belong at all to Eternity. We, living in Time, cannot divest ourselves of its trammels. We cannot conceive of any event without assigning a Time relation to it; without investing it with the trammels and harness and paraphernalia of Time. To us every event must be Past, or Future, with reference to other events. But is there, in reality, any such thing as a Past or a Future? If there is any such thing as Eternity, it now is and always has been and ever must be.

Time is a mere delusion: a false medium, through which we look at things askant. As there can be no such thing as Time in Eternity, there can be no such thing there as a Past or a Future event. If Eternity is anything more than Time exaggerated and extended, — if, indeed, there is any such thing as Eternity, — it is not subject to the laws and conditions of Time. There can be no Past and no Future there; but only an Eternal NOW.

"The absolute truth is not that which we see through a distorting medium of Time, but that which we should see if we were in Eternity and freed from the illusions of Time. To beings who see thus clearly and truthfully, all things must exist in an eternal Present. All things that have been or shall be, *now are*. What we call 'Memory,' is only a mode of consciousness, and to know a Future event is a precisely similar mode of consciousness. Memory and prevision are only different ways of knowing a fact that now is. I see no reason to regard the one as any more truly impossible than the other.

"I grant that in its ordinary Time-clogged state the mind is not capable of discovering those occurrences which to us seem future ones. But it seems to me that there are, or at least may be, conditions of mind in which one rises above the trammels of Time and sees things as they are. Every true poet is at times a prophet by reason of this exaltation of soul. And all the well-attested prophets are poets of the first order."

My friend had no opportunity to finish, nor I to reply to his wire-drawn metaphysics, as we were joined at this stage of the conversation by an acquaintance of the earth earthy, whose talk was of crops.

When he quitted us we were nearing a line of hills to which Bernard directed my attention.

"There!" he exclaimed. "That would make a magnificent battlefield."

I knew his enthusiastic fondness for the study of military history and the details of battles. In common with most other people who have seen nothing of war, I had never been able to picture a battle in my mind; and in reading history I had always found it difficult to comprehend the topographical descriptions of battlefields, or to understand the influence of hill and dale, of copse and stream, upon the issue of a combat. Bernard had mastered the whole subject. He had often moulded in soft earth for my instruction miniature, but exact, representations of many famous battlefields.

The ground we were on was a chain of hills crossing a public thoroughfare, and my friend soon grew enthusiastic in his account of how one army would be posted here, and the other there; how the flanks of each would rest upon certain protected points and how the attacking force would try to carry this or that position.

"If the attacking general knows his business," he said, "he will strain every nerve to drive his adversary from that little knoll there. And if he succeeds in planting a battery or two there, properly supported, his enemy will have to charge him out of the place or reconstruct his own lines, and to reconstruct them will cost him half the value of his position."

A new look came into Bernard's face. The smile had gone from his lips, the great sad look was in his eyes. Gazing at me with intense earnestness, he cried out: "He *must* drive them back. If they once hold that knoll—"

Bernard paused, grew very pale, and then said with some difficulty with his vocal organs: "Let's gallop away from here."

I followed his retreating form, and when we drew rein again, we were a full mile distant from the place of this field lecture. My friend had meantime regained his color and composure, but the old smile had not yet returned to his lips.

"Are you ill, Bernard?" I asked.

"No, I am quite well, thank you."

"Then what—"

"I'll tell you all about it if you won't laugh at me," he said, his lips resuming something of their ordinary expression. "The fact is, all that was prophecy, or prevision, or what you please to call it. While I was explaining an imaginary and possible battle, it became real. THAT BATTLE IS A FACT. I saw the two armies as plainly as I see you, and when the enemy planted that battery there on the hill, driving our forces away, I was among the troops ordered to charge them as a forlorn hope, and *I fell right there, in front of the guns, riddled with canister shot.* I was ahead of the line, for some reason, and just as I fell our men were driven back by a counter-charge right over my body. My friend, prevision is possible. Prevision is a fact. The battle, the charge, the counter-charge, and my death, right there, are what we call Future events. But I know them now as well as I know anything else. I saw it all. I know it for truth."

I was horrified. I tried to draw his mind away from the distressing picture he had conjured up. He seeing my purpose said: "I am not demented, and this doesn't trouble me in the least. It is all fact, but I am not unhappy about it. I turned pale, it is true — any man would with half a dozen canister shot passing through his body. But I am not frightened, not demoralized, and not in the least apprehensive. I don't know when all this is to happen, and as our country is at peace with all the world, I think it is not likely that the battle will come soon. BUT IT WILL COME.

Be sure of that. Now let's talk of something else."

With that he resolutely dismissed the subject, and he never referred to it again.

* * * * *

During the terrible campaign of 1864, the command to which I belonged, after a hard day's march, was sent at ten o'clock at night to take post upon the line.

All night long we lay there expecting the furious onset of the enemy, whose plan it seemed to be to keep us perpetually marching or fighting.

With the early dawn came the battle. And as daylight revealed the features of the newly chosen battlefield, I recognized it as precisely the one that Bernard and I had ridden over several years before. On my right, less than half a mile away, a furious struggle was in progress. I looked and saw our troops driven back from the little eminence on which he and I had stood. The enemy hurried two batteries forward, and planting them there opened a fierce, enfilading fire upon that part of the line in which I stood.

I saw at once that if those batteries should remain there, we must retire and reconstruct our lines. We stood our ground, however, in the hope that the critical position might be recovered. Quickly an attempt was made to that end. A heavy body of infantry was thrown forward with desperate impulse, and straining my eyes with an intensity of eagerness, which I had never felt before, I saw one slender form in advance of the line. A dense volume of powder smoke immediately shut out the view.

When it cleared away the enemy's batteries were still there. Our men had been repulsed. A minute later a second charge was made and it proved successful.

But I knew that I had lost a friend there.

The battle over, I scanned every list of killed and wounded I could find, but could learn nothing of my friend from them. I had every reason to believe that he was not there at all. He had been taken prisoner some months before and paroled. When I had last heard from him he was quietly pursuing his studies at home while waiting for his exchange.

I tried to console myself with this and with the reflection that the partial fulfilment of his prophecy was quite accidental and constituted no reason for assuming its complete fulfilment.

We were on the march or in action all the time, too; and I had plenty of occupation with which to drive depressing thoughts from my mind.

We finally sat down before Petersburg, and the eternity of an eight months' siege began. I was sent to Richmond on some military errand,

THE LAST THAT WAS SEEN OF BERNARD POLAND.

and while there availed myself of the opportunity to visit some friends.

"Where is Bernard?" I asked as lightly as I could, of one who was intimate with his family.

"Haven't you heard?" he replied. "The poor fellow was exchanged in the spring, was elected first lieutenant of a company, and was killed, it is supposed, in one of the battles, I forget which. He was in command of his company, when it was ordered to charge some field batteries on a little hill, and his men say he was last seen ten or a dozen feet in advance of the line, just before a counter-charge drove them back. As the counter-charge was preceded immediately by a volley of canister, the smoke hid him from view. But there seems to be no doubt that he fell there, riddled with canister shot."

A few days later I received a letter from one of Bernard's brother officers, in which, after recapitulating the facts already set forth, he went on to say: "Before we were ordered to the charge, Bernard specially requested me, in the event of his death that day, to write you an exact description of the spot on which he fell. He said, 'He will remember it.' Though what he meant by that, I have never been able to guess. But in loyalty to the love I bore him, I have taken this first opportunity to comply with the last request he made on earth."

The author of that letter who now occupies a prominent position in public life will understand, after reading this sketch, what Bernard meant in saying that I would remember the spot on which he fell.

A BREACH OF ETIQUETTE

WE had marched nearly all night, in order to join Jeb Stuart at the time appointed. This was in the early summer of 1861.

We regarded ourselves with more or less of self-pity, as sleep-sacrificing heroes, who were clearly entitled to a full day's rest.

Jeb Stuart didn't look at it in that way at all. He was a soldier, while we were just beginning to learn how to be soldiers. These things make a difference.

We hadn't got our tents pitched when he ordered us out for a scouting expedition under his personal command.

Our army lay at Winchester. The enemy was at Martinsburg, twenty-two miles away. Stuart, with his four or five hundred horsemen, lay at Bunker Hill, about half-way between but a little nearer to the enemy than to his supports. That was always Stuart's way.

In our scouting expedition that day, we had two or three "brushes" with the enemy — "just to get us used to it," Stuart said.

Finally we went near to Martinsburg, and came upon a farmhouse. The farm gave no appearance of being a large one, or one more than ordinarily prosperous, yet we saw through the open door a dozen or fifteen " farm hands " eating dinner, all of them in their shirt-sleeves.

Stuart rode up, with a few of us at his back, to make inquiries, and we dismounted. Just then a slip of a girl, — not over fourteen, I should say — accompanied by a thick-set, young bulldog, with an abnormal development of teeth, ran up to us.

She distinctly and unmistakably " sicked" that dog upon us. But as the beast assailed us, the young girl ran after him and restrained his ardor by throwing her arms around his neck. As she did so, she kept repeating in a low but very insistent tone to us: "Make 'em put their coats on! Make 'em put their coats on! Make 'em put their coats on!"

Stuart was a peculiarly ready person. He said not one word to the young girl as she led her dog away, but with a word or two he directed a dozen or so of us to follow him with cocked carbines into the dining-room. There he said to the " farm hands": " Don't you know that a gentleman never dines without his coat? Aren't you ashamed of yourselves? And ladies present, too! Get up and put on your coats, every man jack of you, or I'll riddle you with bullets in five seconds."

They sprang first of all into the hallway,

where they had left their arms; but either the bull-dog or the fourteen-year-old girl had taken care of that. The arms were gone. Then seeing the carbines levelled, they made a hasty search of the hiding-places in which they had bestowed their coats. A minute later they appeared as fully uniformed, but helplessly unarmed Pennsylvania volunteers.

They were prisoners of war at once, without even an opportunity to finish that good dinner. As we left the house the young girl came up to Stuart and said: "Don't say anything about it; but the dog wouldn't have bit you. He knows which side *we're* on in this war."

As we rode away this young girl — she of the bull-dog — cried out: "To think the wretches made us give 'em dinner! And in their shirt-sleeves, too!"

THE LADY OF THE GREEN BLIND

THE house looked a little bit odd, but we made allowances for the times, although this was in 1861, soon after the battle of Manassas.

There were seven windows in front, and they all had white shades except one. That one had a dark green Holland blind. We remarked on the fact when the blind was put up, but we thought little of it until we were instructed one day to watch that blind at night and report its doings.

There was a Federal picket post near the house.

We reported many of the performances of that blind without any visible results. But one night it was suddenly drawn entirely down, having before been rolled entirely to the top. When that was reported to the company's headquarters under a tree, a little way in the rear, the captain immediately ordered us to mount.

We rode at a swinging gallop up to the house, and under quietly given orders seized the eleven horses that were tied in the grounds. A moment later a force of dismounted cavalrymen came out of the house with a woman in charge. It was pitch dark, even to us. To men right from the light, and standing within the glare of the doorway, the night must have been absolutely blinding.

We could have shot down the whole detachment without difficulty, but we understood in a moment that there was a woman to be rescued, and in a volley her danger would have been as great as theirs.

We waited therefore for orders.

Then it was that the captain invented a totally new cavalry manœuvre, with a marching command wholly unknown to the books on tactics. He said to us in a low, quiet, but incisive voice: "Form quickly in two single files; advance and split the girl out. I'll take her on my crupper."

It was a pretty manœuvre, and as Charlie rode out between the two single files with the young woman on the crupper, we cheered quite as lustily as we fired. Then we didn't know exactly what to do. We had an appreciation of the fact that Charlie wanted to get the woman out of range as quickly as possible. But we also had a realizing sense, drawn from experience, of Charlie Irving's extreme reluctance to ride away from an enemy who could be faced.

It was Field Mann, the orderly sergeant, who

saw the right way out. He called out to us, in quite unmilitary language: " Don't retreat, boys, Charlie's sure to come back as soon's he's got her safe; meantime we'll fight 'em. Form in line under the cherry trees."

We had them at a disadvantage. They were still in the glare of light from the windows, while we were in the darkness, and we were sixty mounted men to eleven cavalrymen, whose horses had been captured. Moreover we had carbines, and they had none.

By the time we had made an alignment under the trees, and before Field Mann could give another order, the captain came running up on foot, leaped into the saddle of one of the captured horses, and quickly gave a command that completely surrounded the house.

We had those men penned; but just then their comrades at the neighboring picket post discovered that there was trouble on hand, and advanced upon us.

It was an exciting fight there in the darkness and under the trees, so exciting that Stuart quickly sent two other companies to our reinforcement.

At the end of an hour, we marched back with some prisoners; the rest of our foes had scattered and disappeared. When we got to the camp-fires behind the hills, Charlie Irving dismounted, and greeting the lady, who was laboriously mending a torn gown with a hairpin, said: "I hope you managed to ride Selim? He's a demon sometimes, and not at all courteous to ladies. But there was nothing for it but to trust you to him." She murmured something courteous in reply. Then turning with blazing eyes to the Federal officer who had been in command of the party, she asked: "What were you going to do with me, if I hadn't been rescued?"

He replied: "I suppose you would have been hanged as a spy."

And it was true.

After breakfast the next day — I remember that breakfast consisted of some green corn taken from a neighboring field and roasted in the ashes with the husks on, and by the way that's the best way to cook green corn — we escorted the lady back to her home, and under Stuart's orders stationed two cavalry companies in front as a guard.

There is no doubt, I suppose, that the lady was a spy, and that her green window blind had communicated much valuable information.

But no; there was no courtship, no marriage, no honeymoon, no romance, to follow. The lady was forty-five, if a day; and besides that, Irving was already engaged to a girl down South.

YOUNGBLOOD'S LAST MORNING

WE were all well used to seeing men shot, but this was different.

It was a soft, warm, mellow autumn morning. It was a day suggestive of all gentleness. A purple, Indian-summer haze enveloped the earthworks and the camps. Nature had issued an invitation to peace and repose. The cannon were not at work. Nobody on either side had been tempted to bombard anybody else. Even the mortars and the sharp-shooters were still.

It was not the kind of morning for the bloody work of war.

Yet a young man was to be killed within the hour. He was to be killed deliberately, in cold blood, by sentence of a court-martial, and with great pomp and ceremony; and nobody, even in his heart, could say nay to the justice of the sentence.

For Youngblood had done an infamous thing.

There were many desertions to the enemy about that time. The war was manifestly drawing to a close, and men who lacked self-sacrificing devotion were getting tired of its hardships and privations. In order to stop these desertions, orders had been issued that any soldier arresting another in the act of going to the enemy should have a thirty days' furlough.

Youngblood was on picket one day with another man. He proposed to that other man that they both should desert, and they started together toward the enemy's lines. According to Youngblood's story, it was his purpose to arrest his comrade, and thus earn a furlough at the expense of the other fellow's life. Whether this story was true or not doesn't much matter. The other fellow arrested him.

In any case, he deserved to pay the penalty he did. He was tried, convicted, and sentenced. The sentence was approved by all the authorities, including the war department. This morning it was to be carried out.

It was about ten o'clock, Youngblood's regiment was formed into three sides of a hollow square. Near the entrance to the square, on the right, rested Youngblood's coffin. Beside it was Youngblood's grave.

Presently an ambulance drove up, bearing the prisoner and his attendant guards. As he stepped lightly and lithely from the ambulance, we saw him to be a fine specimen of young manhood. He was twenty-three or twenty-four years of age; tall, well built, and full of elastic vigor. He was handsome, too, and of refined and gentle countenance.

There was no sign of flinching in him: nothing that denoted the coward which his explanation of his crime had shown him to be.

It seemed something more than a pity to put a fellow like that to death.

He took his place in front of the guards and just in rear of the band, and the dead march began.

He walked alone.

Slowly, and with cadenced step, the procession moved around inside the square. And as it passed me, I was curious to observe the condemned man's behavior. His step was as steady and as firm as that of any man in the guard. I looked at his hands to see if there were any convulsive clutching of the fingers. There was none. I doubt if any man in all that regiment felt so calm in mind or so well poised in nerve as Youngblood looked.

Having completed the seemingly endless march around the three closed sides of the square, the procession turned to the right, and crossed its open end to the point of execution.

There an officer stepped forward and read to Youngblood the findings and sentence of the court which had condemned him, with the formal endorsements approving them and ordering the sentence executed. The guard which

Youngblood's Last Morning

had the prisoner in charge divided to the right and left, and Youngblood was left standing alone in front of his coffin, and beside his open grave.

At the word of command he knelt upon the coffin and folded his arms across his chest. Again at the word of command twelve soldiers stepped out in front of him with guns in their hands. Six of these guns carried ball cartridges, and six were blank. No man in the firing squad was permitted to know whether his gun had a bullet in it or not.

The officer in command spoke scarcely above his breath, but so hushed was the time that his words were audible to the three thousand men there assembled, as he said to each alternate man: "Fire at his head," and to the intervening man: "Fire at his chest." Then turning his back, which was perhaps not an officer-like thing to do, the lieutenant gave in a husky voice the word of command.

"Ready, aim, fire."

There was a sharp crack from twelve rifles fired simultaneously. There was a whirr and whistle of six bullets that had passed through the head or chest of the doomed man, and hurtled off into the fields beyond. Army rifles fire with tremendous force.

The dead man's body rose to its feet and fell limply forward.

Five minutes later all that was left of Youngblood was buried beneath six feet of earth.

There was no merriment in any of the camps that day, or the next, or the next. Even our scant rations were not much relished by those of us who had witnessed this scene.

And yet, as I said at the beginning, we were all well used to seeing men killed.

BILLY GOODWIN

I NEVER have known whether Billy Goodwin was a brave man or not.

He was certainly not afraid of anything; but the absence of fear from his composition was so complete that I was always in doubt whether he was entitled to credit for never yielding to that emotion.

His fearlessness seemed like the color of his sandy hair and his pale blue eyes — something over which he had no control.

At Cold Harbor, in 1864, when an artillery duel was going on, plus a tremendous sharpshooter fire, Billy, with his back to the enemy, lazily lounged upon the breastworks. All the rest of us were crouching behind them.

I remember as an incident that he was eating a sandwich. It was composed of two halves of a hard-tack biscuit and a slice of raw pickled pork — his entire rations for the day. He was carefully holding his hand under his chin, in order to save all the crumbs. We weren't wasting crumbs in those days.

A lieutenant, who had already been mentioned in orders for gallantry, cautiously pushed up his head to peer over the breastworks on which Goodwin was sitting. Billy placed his hand upon the prematurely bald head of the lieutenant, shoved him down, and said: "Keep below the dirt, or you'll get a bullet through your billiard ball. Don't you know this is no time to be exposing yourself?"

I have elsewhere celebrated Billy. In doing so I have suggested that, while he had a high sense of personal duty, he had no sense whatever of personal danger.

On that terrible 30th of August, 1864, when the mine was exploded at Petersburg, Goodwin was detailed to act as courier for General Lee and General Beauregard.

A Northern negro soldier had broken somehow out of the crater and through the lines. He rushed madly into headquarters. He struck frantically at General Lee with his bayonet. General Beauregard parried the blow with his sword. The negro turned and ran out of the door. Beauregard, in his excitement, called out to Goodwin, "Go and kill that man!"

Stepping quickly, as was his custom, Billy gave pursuit. A few moments later he returned. He presented himself in all his superb length of limb. He gave the military salute to General Beauregard. When that officer asked:

"What is it, orderly?" Billy replied: "I beg respectfully to report that I have killed that man in accordance with orders."

That was Billy. As a soldier he was a good kind. He obeyed all orders without questioning them. He did all his duties as he understood them. But, as I have said, I have never been able to determine whether he was really a brave man, or whether he was merely a man so constituted as to be insensible to personal danger.

But I will say this for Billy, which may help to decide this point,—

We were marching from Spottsylvania to Cold Harbor. We marched for fifty-six hours at the double quick. Now and then we had to fight at the quadruple quick. We had no food. We had no sleep. We had no rest.

Near the end of this tremendous strain Billy came to me under a tree, where I was snatching a five minutes' repose. He said, with an air of great mystery: "I've got a coon for my mess. I bought it of a nigger back there. So I don't want this piece of corn-bread. I wish you'd take it. I know you're hungry."

We did not readily accept food from each other in those days, lest we starve each other.

I struggled to resist this proffer, but Billy insisted on that coon as satisfying all his personal wants. At last, therefore, I accepted the three or four ounces of powder-grimed cornbread which he pressed upon me.

I learned afterwards that Billy had lied. There wasn't any coon.

MANASSAS

I CALL it Manassas.
That is the name we Southerners gave it. We won that battle more completely and more conspicuously than any other battle was won by either side during the Civil War.

It is the right of the victor always to name the action. We named it Manassas. In the North it is called Bull Run.

We reached Manassas after two days and nights of ceaseless marching, at ten o'clock on the evening of the 20th of July, 1861.

We knew that trouble was at hand; otherwise Stuart would not have swung us at such a breakneck speed across the mountains from the valley to this point. We were six hundred strong.

Six hundred young Virginians, cradled in the saddle, and who had shot wild turkeys as soon as we were able to digest them. There was another battalion of cavalry present, under Colonel Radford, numbering perhaps three hundred men. But the story had gone forth in the Northern army that we were thirty thousand of the finest horsemen ever known since the days of the Mamelukes.

That story had its part in creating the panic at Manassas.

I believe we were good horsemen. There were men among us who might have given the Mamelukes points, both in horsemanship and in the use of the sabre. But if our nine hundred men had been the thirty thousand reported, we should have thundered into Washington on the night of Sunday, July 21, 1861, and would have ended the war then and there, in spite of the presidential stupidity which feared that "aggression" might anger a people with whom we were at war.

We lay that night in an open field, each man having his horse tethered to his left arm, and each man booted, spurred, sabred, and pistolled for instant action.

The bugle sounded no reveille that morning. A shell from the enemy's camp, which fell in the midst of the regiment, saved the bugler the trouble.

With a laugh, which was almost a chuckle, Stuart called out: "That's 'boots and saddles,' boys," and in an instant we were on our horses.

The first great battle of the war had begun.

It was not until noon, or nearly that, that the cavalry had any real work to do. I didn't look at my watch, but it must have been about noon when Stuart swept us at a tremendous pace through a regiment or two of Zouaves, and back again over the same ground. I saw no Zouaves for the reason that there was too much dust to see anything; but it was understood when the charge was over, that we had driven them back. And half a dozen empty saddles in our own ranks attested the fact that they had not been driven back without a stubborn and manly resistance.

A little later, we cavalrymen were ordered up to the support of some batteries that had temporarily run out of ammunition. Our reputation as Mamelukes sufficed at that point to prevent a charge, so that our real work in the battle did not begin until the panic in McDowell's army set in.

Then Stuart rose in his stirrups and shouted at the top of his voice: "They're licked, boys! They're licked! They're licked!"

Then hastily he rattled off orders. The substance of them was that we were to divide the cavalry into squads of ten and twenty men each, and proceed at once in pursuit.

"If there aren't officers, and non-commissioned officers enough, let anybody command a squad. This is business."

As the several squads started at a gallop after the enemy, Stuart called out to each:

"Attack any force you find. There is no cohesion left among 'em."

In that command he struck the key-note of the whole situation. Seasoned soldier that he was, he knew that without cohesion, soldiers are helpless, and numbers count for nothing.

We plunged forward across every ford and along every road that led from Bull Run towards Centreville. At every point we found "chaos come again."

A squad of ten men, armed only with sabres and pistols, but backed by the Mameluke tradition, would call out to eighty or a hundred fully armed infantry: "Throw down your arms, or we'll put you to the sword! Throw down your arms, or we'll put you to the sword!"

The panic-stricken men would obey the order instantly, disregarding the fact that with a single volley they might have swept the insolent squad instantly out of existence.

It was not merely that the army was panic stricken. It was encumbered at every step by a multitude of embarrassing picnickers, — a multitude of men and women who had come out from Washington to see us exterminated and to join in a triumphal march to Richmond. These people had brought out with them more superfluous provisions than our army had eaten for a fortnight. They abandoned their luxuries in the middle of the road and ran. They left champagne enough unopened for a regiment to swim in. They fled precipitately, adding at every step by their own insensate fear to the panic that had already overtaken the troops.

Men cut horses out of vehicles that held helpless women, and madly mounting them abandoned their charges and their duties, in order to escape a present and impending danger to themselves. Fortunately for their charges, the Southerners were not making war on women.

Every woman was instantly assured of her own personal safety. Every horse that was left behind was hitched at once to a vehicle, and the vehicle loaded with women was started under an assurance of safe conduct towards Washington. When the supply of abandoned horses fell short, it was made good by animals from our batteries, and now and then by the riderless horse of one of the Mamelukes who had received a mortal wound.

Along the roads we found many dead men, for whose deaths no coroner would have been able to account — men utterly destitute of wounds, who had died clearly either of fright, or of exhaustion, or of both.

At Cub Run, an ambulance or a caisson broke down on the bridge and obstructed it. The obstruction almost instantly caused a congestion of two or three thousand panic-stricken soldiers and picnickers on the hither side of the stream.

Then came Kemper with his guns. He was as black as a negro with powder smoke. His cannoneers were equally begrimed. From the top of a hill, not more than two hundred yards distant, — pistol-shot range, — he opened fire with canister. The effect upon the crowd was instantaneous and almost startling. Its constituent members dispersed as a covey of partridges does when a shot-gun is fired into its lurking place. Some of them ran up the creek. Some of them ran down the creek. Some of them plunged into the creek, and crossed or drowned, as the case may be.

It was just then that Stuart rode up and cried out: "We'll go into Washington to-night, boys. And my headquarters will be at Willard's Hotel."

It was just then also that couriers came, bearing the paralyzing presidential order to stop the pursuit at Cub Run.

It was just then that the despondency of the Mamelukes began.

A little later it rained.

MY LAST NIGHT ON PICKET

MY period of service in the cavalry was about to expire. I was not tired of the cavalry service; on the contrary, I was very much in love with it. Any full-blooded man must have been so under such leadership as Stuart's.

But for reasons pertaining to Joe, I had sought and obtained a transfer to the artillery.

Joe was just sixteen.

The infantry regiment in which he had gone out had been so cut to pieces in a fierce fight that it was dissolved. Joe and a bullet-riddled flag were about all there was left of it.

Therefore Joe had enlisted in a battery of artillery. He was as brave a fellow as is made, and as cantankerous and self-assertive as a brave boy is apt to be. I felt it necessary to be with him to keep him from being unnecessarily killed or court-martialled, and to exercise over him that mature, paternal influence which the superior age of twenty-one justified.

This was my last night of cavalry service. It was late autumn in 1861. The company was ordered on picket at Fairfax Court House. The enemy was very urgent just then, and gave us a good deal of trouble on the picket lines.

I was ordered to a post underneath a very broad and low spreading tree, so that when I sat upon my horse I was not visible from the thicket in front, and would not have been even if it had been broad daylight.

That thicket was full of sharp-shooters, and when I went on post about seven o'clock in the evening, I was instructed to preserve absolute silence in self-protection, and warned that it would probably not be possible to relieve me until morning.

My mare was a restless creature at ordinary times, but she had learned the whole art of picket duty. If I had been anywhere else, she would have champed the bit, and pawed the ground, and snorted in her restlessness. Standing there at night, with a bullet whistling over her head every minute or two, she was as still as the traditional mouse.

I sat there all night on her back with pistols drawn, and in a silence such as nobody but a picket thus placed ever maintains.

Just as the day was dawning, or rather just as the gray in the eastern sky began to suggest the possibility of dawn, a sergeant crawling on his belly approached me from the rear. In a whisper I called out, "Who goes there?" He, also in a whisper, let me know his identity. He had come to order my withdrawal from the post.

Not until we had reached a point a hundred yards in the rear was anything further said. There I found the company drawn up in line with Charlie Irving at its head.

"Many shots from the thicket?" asked Charlie.

"Two or three to the minute," I answered, "throughout the night."

"All right," he replied, "we'll scoop those fellows in; they're getting to be obnoxious."

Then in a low tone he told us precisely what we were to do, and we were to do it without further orders. He was to lead, of course, but he wanted to give as few commands as possible, in order to make his movement successful.

Silently we moved off over the soft turf to the left. Crossing the road below the thicket we struck a gallop and quickly surrounded the space occupied by the sharp-shooters. It was the work of but a few minutes to close in upon and capture them. Two of our saddles were emptied in the operation, and five of the sharp-shooters were left unburied in the brush; the rest we took with us to headquarters, another company having replaced us on picket.

Among the prisoners was one little fellow, apparently not over fifteen or sixteen years of age. His features were clear cut and delicate and his clothing was worn as if it had belonged to somebody else.

When we had got well to the rear and the daylight was broad, Charlie Irving looked at the little fellow and said: "How old are you, my boy?"

"Twenty-two," he replied, "but I'm a girl."

That girl was sent back under a flag of truce. We didn't know what else to do with her.

GRIFFITH'S CONTINUED STORY

IT was in the early summer of 1864. We were in the trenches at Spottsylvania.

It had been raining continuously all day, with now and then a heavy downpour, just to remind us that a little rain ought not to matter to old soldiers. By the use of fragments of fence rail and such other sticks as we could secure to stand upon, we managed to avoid sinking below our ankles into the soft, red, Virginian mud.

It was a little after two o'clock in the morning, but we were all awake and on duty. For it was not General Grant's purpose at that time to allow us much of repose. We had stood in the trenches and in the rain all day, and we must stand in the trenches and in the rain all night, and as much longer as it might please the enemy to keep us there.

The night was one of the blackest I have ever known. There was no possibility of sending couriers anywhere, and all orders had, therefore, to be passed from mouth to mouth up and down the lines.

Every few minutes a great downpour of bucketfuls would come; and, worse still, every now and then the enemy would rush forward in the darkness and come upon us at pistol-shot range without notice.

It was Ulysses S. Grant we were fighting, and that was the line on which he was going to "fight it out, if it took all summer."

We felt the need of entertainment, so somebody called out to a sergeant: "Tell us a story."

"No, no," said Johnny Garrett, "let Griffith tell a story, for he never finishes, and this is a long night."

The suggestion was applauded and insisted upon. Whether Griffith blushed or not, it was much too dark to see; but after a little chaffing he consented to tell the story. Just as he began Billy Goodwin, who always wanted to gamble on everything, offered to bet three to one that he would never finish.

"Shut up, Goodwin," said Johnny Garrett, "and let him begin, anyhow. If he don't get through by the middle of the night, I'll negotiate the bet with you."

Thereupon Griffith began.

"Well, 'taint much of a story — only a bear story."

"Bet two to one he never gets to the bear," said the incorrigible Goodwin.

"Be quiet, will you?" cried some one at the

right of the company. The man next to him mistook this adjuration for a command sent down the line; so, to the astonishment of everybody to the left of us, the word was passed from mouth to mouth: "*Be quiet, will you! Be quiet, will you! Be quiet, will you!*"

"Well," said Griffith, "'twas about six year ago, or maybe seven. No, lemme see — 'twas the same year that Jim Coffee married Mirandy Adams. Must have been eight year ago, I s'pose."

Just then came the order down the line: "Perfect silence! Enemy advancing!"

The next minute a line of bayonets broke out of the fog in front of us, and a flaring fire blazed forth in our faces. The charge upon us was a determined one, and for full three minutes it required all our efforts to repel it. After that the artillery silenced all conversation by pouring a shower of shot and shell into the retiring assailants.

"Still ready to make that bet," said Billy Goodwin. But Griffith began again undaunted. He was a phlegmatic person, whose mind was never driven from its not very large purposes by any shock — even that of a shower of canister.

"Well, as I wuz a-sayin', it wuz about six or eight year ago — it don't really matter, I s'pose, how long ago it wuz — "

"No," said Billy Goodwin, "let her rip."

"Well, as I wuz a-sayin'—" Just then the enemy charged again.

Griffith had captured a Henry rifle two days before, in the battle of the Wilderness, and it was loaded with fourteen ball cartridges. With that deliberation which characterized him in everything, he delivered those fourteen shots in the face of the enemy, who by that time had retired. Then he turned and began to fill the magazine of his rifle again, saying: "Well, you see, as I wuz a-sayin', Peter Coffee he taken a cawntract for a bridge over Tye River. Now Peter always pertended that he knew how to lay out bridge work. Of course I knew better. I'd been to Fletcher Massie's school with him, and I knew just how little 'rithmetic he knew. Fletch, he carried me through the rule o' three, and you can't lay out bridge work till you've *bin* through the rule o' three."

The day was dawning, and just then came an order for us to move to the right, the extreme right, four or five miles away. We marched at once. Grant was making his celebrated move by the left flank.

When we got into position, it was necessary to throw up such earthworks as we could with our bayonets, using fence rails for revetments. This occupied us during most of the day, and scattered as we were, we were not able to listen to the remainder of Griffith's story.

Griffith's Continued Story

That afternoon, to our surprise, we received a ration of three-quarters of a pound of flour to each man. When we had baked it, I happened to go by Tom Booker's position and saw him eating the entire cake. Tom looked at me pitifully as I remonstrated with him for eating three days' rations in advance, and he said with tears in his voice if not in his eyes: "I know it, but I'm go'n' t' fill my stomach once, if I starve for it. I *wish* I was a woman or a baby."

A few minutes later came the order to move; our battery was at that time unhorsed. It had been planned to leave it in the rear, because its guns could not be moved for lack of horses, but with one voice the men had demanded the privilege of taking rifles and going with the battalion as sharp-shooters.

On this march the battalion was the rear guard of the army, and our rifle-armed battery was the rear guard of the battalion.

For fifty-six hours we marched without food or sleep, pausing every fifteen minutes to fight awhile, and then double-quicking to catch up.

There was no chance for Griffith in all this. But when we got to Cold Harbor, and went into the works, Billy Goodwin at a favorable moment insisted that he should resume his story.

"You see I've got three bets on it," said Billy.

Just then a grape-shot passed through George Campbell's foot, and distracted our attention for a time. Then came General Field, who ordered us to burn a barn in front that was full of sharp-shooters. The first two or three shots from the battalion did the business. The sharp-shooters ran with all their might across a thousand yards of space, while we poured upon them the sharpest rifle fire we could deliver. Some of them got to cover, and some of them didn't.

It was not till we moved to Bottom's Bridge that Griffith had a chance to resume his story. There we were all sick from having eaten boiled potato vines, for lack of other food. Being too ill to go to sleep, we demanded a continuation of the story.

"Well, as I wuz a-sayin'," said Griffith, "I'd gone clean through the rule o' three in Fletch Massie's school, and Peter Coffee he knew it. As I told yuh, he'd taken the cawntract to lay out this bridge work; so he got his wife to write to me to come up and do the 'rithmetic. Well, just as I wuz startin' up, Bill Linsey says to me, — you know he kept a store down there at Arrington, he says to me, says he, 'Griffith, there's a runlet o' cider that's got twenty gallon in it. Can you lif' it?' I says, 'Yes, I can lif' it and drink out o' the bung, if you'll let me drink es much es I please.' I lifted it and took a big swallow of the sweet stuff, then I says, 'I can carry it up the mountain,' says I, and he says,

says he, 'On your back?' says he, an' I says, 'Yes, on my back,' says I. An' he says, says he, 'Well, you can have it ef you'll agree to carry it up the mountain on your back, and not take no lift frum nobody.'"

Just then a battery, three thousand yards away, opened on us, and we had to run to cover, every man of us with his hands on his stomach, in physical memory of the potato vines. Our guns were not in position, and all we could do was to ensconce ourselves behind big trees. As the artillery fire kept up, General Alexander rode to this point of the lines and ordered up three batteries of rifled cannon; by the time they had finished their little controversy with the enemy, we had recovered from the potato tops sufficiently to go to sleep. So Griffith's story was to be "continued in our next."

Our "next" came only after we got to Petersburg. There our battery took charge of the mortars of the army. Griffith was one of the men I selected when asked to volunteer for a particularly perilous mortar service. He might or might not be able to tell a story, but he could stand fire as well as any man I ever knew.

About four o'clock one morning, when we had been engaged in a fierce bombardment all night, the fire ceased for a time, and Billy Goodwin demanded the rest of that bear story.

"You see I've got seven bets on that story," said Billy, "and I don't want to win any man's money unfairly. One bet is that he won't ever get to the bear, and I don't want to take any man's money without givin' him a chance."

"Well, wait a minute," I replied, "till I start up the fire; we've got to have some breakfast."

The fire was out.

"Somebody must go up," I said, "to the next fort and get a chunk of fire. It won't do to get fire by shooting a mortar," — which was our usual way, — "because if we do that, we'll start this bombardment again."

"I'll go," said Griffith, "and then I'll tell the rest of that story."

There was a fearful hail of bullets between the two forts. The cannon were silent, but the musketry fire was incessant. Griffith started off, crouching as he went up the path so as to expose as little as possible of his person.

That was the last I ever saw of him.

As he was borne off on the litter, he sent word to me that he "hoped I hadn't any bets on that bear story."

A CHEERFUL SUPPER OF CHEERS

AS Commissary it was Haskell's business to see to it that we had plenty to eat; but the seven days' fights below Richmond were on, and Haskell was, first of all, a fighter, — a thing uncommon in Commissaries and Quartermasters.

Instead of attending to his pork and meal wagons in the rear, he went to the front.

There he was active in a degree that commanded the respect of his general. He interested himself so much in the movements of troops, and in the controversy with the enemy, that he forgot all about the wagons.

In this service he had his right arm shot off by a cannon-ball.

When night came, and we wanted something to eat, there was a good deal of growling because we had nothing. But when the story was told of how our Commissary had fought, and how he had lost an arm in the fighting, a fellow with more humor than appetite got up and cried: "I move that we sup on three cheers and a tiger for the Commissary that fights."

The three cheers were given.

As soon as his wound was healed, Haskell was made a major and placed in command of the battalion.

There may have been many better Commissaries than Haskell, but there were no better fighting majors.

HOW THE TAR HEELS STUCK

THE sergeant-major sat there on his horse in the drenching rain. There was nothing to do but to endure. The three days of fighting in the Wilderness in that early summer of 1864, and the three nights of sleeplessness had considerably undone his nerves.

But for the first time in his life he realized that he had a hope at least for an opportunity. He had a lieutenant's command. He hoped for a chance to make himself a lieutenant, in fact. With two guns, twenty-six men, and twenty-four horses under his command, and wholly detached from his battery, he had hope, that gray foggy morning, that he might have an opportunity. Yet here he was, standing behind a hill, soaking wet, and with no apparent prospect.

Three times the infantry had been ordered forward to the top of that hill. Three times they had been swept away as with a broom.

The hill was clearly untenable.

Then came General Alexander.

"Have you nerve, courage, backbone? Do you want an opportunity?"

The sergeant-major answered, "Yes."

"Then take your guns to the top of that hill and STAY THERE."

The sergeant-major gave the necessary orders, and advanced at once, feeling that he and his men were lambs sent to the slaughter.

When he appeared on top of the hill, twenty batteries and ten thousand riflemen opened upon him. But his orders were to "stay there," and the sergeant-major wanted to be a lieutenant.

His horse sank under him at the first fire. His men went down like grass before the scythe.

But he STAYED THERE.

About that time a North Carolina general rode up to his brigade and called aloud: "Men, are you going to allow these guns to be captured? They say we North Carolinians have tar on our heels; let's show them that tar *sticks*. Forward! March!"

Five minutes later that hill was occupied by three thousand North Carolinians, the tar on whose heels STUCK. Half a dozen more batteries were ordered up, and the young sergeant-major was directed to move his guns by hand to the rear.

By hand. Because of his twenty-four horses only two remained alive; while there were only thirteen left out of his twenty-six men to handle the guns by hand. This is what we called "life" in the Confederate army.

"LITTLE LAMKIN'S BATTERY"

FOR twenty-four hours I had had a man on my mind.

He had been court-martialled and was sentenced to be shot. He was in the guardhouse.

I know of no good reason why I should have objected to his execution; he certainly deserved all that he was to get. But I had been his counsel before the court-martial, and it is never a pleasant thing for a lawyer to have his client executed.

He belonged officially to me. I had assumed a responsibility for him, and I felt that it would not be fully discharged if he should be led out and shot.

I had known Beavers for a very brief time; but as his counsel I had learned much from him in confidence as to his career. He was a person of elective affinities. It was his habit to desert. He had served on both sides and in many capacities. He always fought well on whichever side he might happen to be serving. As a gambler, he always "played his game for all it was worth."

Why he had deserted back and forth in this

way without any cogent reason, I never knew. I used to think sometimes that he had done so at first just to try how a new style and color of uniform might suit his particular kind of beauty. His beauty was not in itself conspicuous.

I learned from him incidentally that his various reasons for desertion from one side to the other had not been of a kind that would have controlled the action of a less fastidious man.

On one occasion he had deserted because he smelt mutton from the camp-kettles of the enemy. He had a predilection for mutton.

I learned that he returned to us once, because one night, when he was not quite himself, a comrade had put him to bed and reversed the order of his blankets. Beavers explained to me with great particularity that a certain gray blanket had been placed on top of a certain brown one. He could not be expected to remain with a regiment under such conditions.

At last he had been caught in the act of deserting. He had been tried, and, in spite of such legal acumen as I could bring to bear, had been convicted, sentenced, and the next day but one was to be shot.

Now that he was sure to die, he seemed to make no more of the fact than of any other indifferent thing. I do not mean that he was careless of his fate. He took everything seriously. But facts were to him facts, and he did not worry over them. He did not think it worth while.

So when he was sentenced to death, he adjusted his blankets in the proper order so that he might not have a nightmare, and slept the sleep of the contented.

With all my contempt for Beavers I was sorry that he was to die. There was something in the reckless character of the man that appealed to me. Something that made me feel that it was a pity that this abundant life should be extinguished by a rifle shot.

I had been thinking all night. I had thought of every argument in his favor. I had searched my mind to see if any point had been neglected. Early in the night I had gone to Beavers, and asked him for the aid of suggestion — suggestion that might lead to information. But here again his habits balked me. He said: "I'm gambling in this case on your brains."

I might myself have been willing to do that, but I was gambling with Beavers's life for a stake.

Beavers was of course just that kind of man, whom a self-respecting person feels it his duty to despise; but somehow I could not quite despise Beavers. His coolness appealed to me strongly. His bravado seemed a sort of bravery. His readiness to meet the consequences, and pay the penalties of his own misdeeds, was a thing hard to distinguish from heroism.

He had no principles, of course. He did not pretend to have any. But he had certain methods of thought which seemed to serve him in lieu of principles.

It was just before dawn. I had not slept. As I lay in my tent with the flaps thrown back, all that was discernible was the rather spectral-looking tented city with its precise white rows. I had become so nervous, staring through the dark at the place where I knew the tent pole to be, that at last I turned out for good. I tightened my belt. It was our habit to sleep in our clothes — for reasons.

The first gray of the morning touched the camp, and looking down the row I saw a fragile figure moving from one tent to another, and pausing occasionally in uncertainty. At first I could not be certain whether it was a woman or not. Finally the figure straightened up and stood looking towards the guardhouse; it was that of a woman.

I had not seen a woman in two months.

The camp was silent with that quietude that is so impressive just before the dawn.

After staring at the guardhouse for a moment, while I stood staring at her, the woman turned her eyes and we stood looking at each other. After halting a moment she came staggering up the narrow lane between the two rows of tents, making a peculiar, nervous movement with her hands, but saying nothing. She stood for a few moments a little way from the tent door, clasping and unclasping her hands.

I saw that she was ill. She reeled up against the tent pole, and would have fallen had I not caught her by the arm. I seated her on a log, all the seat there was. After a moment she revived a little, and said in a faint voice, "Beavers."

At that moment reveille sounded. The woman was too evidently ill for me to leave her. I sent a sergeant to attend the roll-call. I directed our cook to provide the woman with coffee and food.

Then I questioned her a little. She had walked twenty-two miles over railroad ties.

She was Beavers's wife.

She said to me: "You are his counsel, I believe?"

"Yes," I replied, "and I have done everything I could to save him."

"No, you have not," she answered. "You have not made the point that he was never legally enlisted as a soldier, I'll warrant! He's over forty-five and can't be conscribed. He was pardoned out of the penitentiary on condition that he should enlist, but the court-martial had no proof of that. There's nothing whatever to show that he's a soldier; and if he ain't a soldier, he can't be punished for desertion. I've come to tell you, for he would never think of it."

I jumped to my feet. I called a sentinel, and told him to take the woman to the guardhouse and make her as comfortable as possible. I mounted my horse and galloped to the station. I roused the telegraph operator two hours before his time. He was a sleepy fellow, but he was accustomed to taking imperative messages out of hours. I gave him this one to the war department: —

Beavers to be shot to-morrow morning. No proof whatever he was ever soldier. If not soldier, could not have deserted. Too old for conscript law, and no proof of enlistment except Governor Letcher's telegram. Telegram not under oath, not legal testimony. Witness not subjected to cross-examination. As counsel, I demand stay in this man's case.

I rode back to the guardhouse, and found that a new member had been added to the battery. The company was known as Lamkin's Battery.

We named the new member "*Little* Lamkin's Battery," to distinguish it, I suppose, from the big one.

Beavers sat all that morning with his wife's hand in his, and Little Lamkin's Battery in his arms.

He said it looked like its mother. He'd "gamble on that."

Not until within an hour of the time appointed for Beavers's execution did there come a reply from the war department. But when it came it was thoroughly satisfactory. It read thus:—

> Legal points conclusive. Release Beavers and restore him to duty. Duplicate sent to General Walker.

Soon after that Beavers deserted, blankets and all, to "the other enemy"— that was his form of speech, not mine.

The next time I saw him was under peculiar circumstances.

In July, 1865, I went on board the steamer *Morning Star*, at Portland, four miles below Louisville, Kentucky.

I was two or three hours in advance of the sailing of the boat. Only a few people were scattered about the front of the cabin. I went to the clerk, paid for my room and passage, and pocketed thirty dollars in change. A moment later the porter came in with my trunk. I put my hand in my vest pocket to get the dollar due him, but found my thirty dollars gone.

I had all the feelings which a man always has when he finds that his pocket has been picked — which include the feeling of helplessness.

There was on board a brigade of troops going South. They were late enlisters, who had seen none of the fighting. The men were on the deck below, of course. The officers, though their transportation orders called only for deck passage, were by courtesy permitted in the cabin. There were a dozen or twenty of them, mainly rough lumbermen, or something of that kind. They evidently wanted to see a fight. So they concluded to pick that fight with me.

One of them came up to me where I was reading a novel, and began the trouble by saying: "You're a rebel."

"No," I replied. "I was a rebel while the rebellion lasted, but I have taken the oath of allegiance, and am at present a loyal citizen of the United States."

"Well, you *were* a rebel," he said, with more offence in his tone than in his words; "and I want to know what you are doing here in the North."

"I'm not in the North," I replied; "but in the middle of a river that separates the North from the South."

By this time half a dozen others of the crowd had gathered in front of me with angry faces. It was manifestly their purpose to make trouble, and I saw no use in trying to ward it off. They were planning a fight; and whether it was to be a safe one or not, it seemed to me a good time to begin it.

I sprang to my feet and faced them. I was utterly unarmed, while they carried their weapons. I grasped a chair as the only means of defence at hand, and with remarks which are better not repeated, perhaps, told them to come on.

Just at that moment a stateroom door opened behind me, and two warm hands thrust two pistols into my grasp. The next moment a stalwart figure, armed in the same way, stood beside me, and, presenting two pistols, called out: "Hands up, gentlemen! The first man that moves dies. You're twenty to two of us, but —"

Some language followed.

The men threw up their hands.

Without taking his eyes off his adversaries or lowering his weapons, my comrade called out: "Mr. Clerk, send for the captain."

When the captain came, my comrade reported that these men had made an unwarranted assault upon an inoffensive passenger, and said: "They have no business in the cabin, anyway. As a first-class passenger, I call on you to send 'em below, where they belong."

The captain was willing enough. He had been three times arrested during the war for aiding "rebel sympathizers." A minute later these officers had become deck passengers.

Then I turned to my deliverer, and to my

astonishment he was Beavers. He had grown stout, and was resplendent in a suit of clothes with checks so broad that it might easily have taken two persons to show the pattern; otherwise he was the same old nonchalant, reckless Beavers, ready to gamble upon any chance and to pay his losses though the payment might be with his life.

I made my identity known to him of course. He replied immediately: " Why, of course, I reckonized you long before this thing occurred, and I have been trying to get an excuse for speaking to you. Because you see when you came aboard in mufti I didn't know who you was, and so I lifted thirty dollars out of your clothes. I wouldn't have done it if I'd a' known it was you, and now I want to hand it back. I could just as easily have picked that other fellow's pocket — the one that picked the quarrel with you. I never go back on my friends, never! And I've never forgot how you got me out of that scrape."

He handed me back the thirty dollars and I thanked him. He said: "Don't mention it." He added, though I never knew what he meant by it: " I'll square the whole thing with that other feller. He's got more'n thirty dollars in *his* wad."

I naturally felt a little warm towards Beavers. I owed him my life. Therefore when he suggested some alcoholic celebration of the incident I compromised on a cigar. However little you may esteem a man, it is difficult to snub him a few minutes after he has saved your life.

Beavers went to the baggage-master and said something to him which I didn't hear. The baggage-master shook his head in dissent.

"Oh, that's all right," said Beavers; "it's five dollars to you, old man."

"Oh, well, that's different," said the baggage-master, and two minutes later Beavers was searching one of his trunks. Presently he came up with a wad of papers in his hand and we returned to the cabin. There he spread out some architectural designs for a gorgeous monument, and said: "Look at that. That's the design of the monument I've just put up over that wife of mine. She was a mighty good sort, and I've spent good money to give her a proper send-off. I've paid five thousand dollars to the architect for the design, and fifteen thousand dollars to have it built. You see business is good with me just now. I've got a faro bank at Louisville and another at Evansville and two at Cairo, and another at St. Louis, and three at Memphis and one at Vicksburg, and two at New Orleans. As for me I *run the river and make what there is in it.*"

Suddenly a thought occurred to him.

"By the way," he said, "you remember

about Little Lamkin's Battery? Well, he's on board." Beckoning to a negro nurse, he said: "Bring that little rascal here."

A few minutes later the nurse returned, having a peculiarly bright, three-year-old boy in charge, whom I greeted as an old friend. After talking with the little chap for a few moments I turned to Beavers and said: "What are you going to make out of him, Beavers?"

"Something better than his father is," he replied, "for his mother's sake ; and that reminds me you're just out of the war and you've got your way to make. It won't do for you to know *me*. If you ever meet me goin' up and down the river, I'll cut you dead and don't you say nothing."

CURRY

CURRY was our mess cook.
He was a great rascal, but one of the best cooks in the world. And besides he was discriminative in his rascality. He never did any dishonest thing towards us; but he was capable of any conceivable crime, if he could commit it in our behalf.

He was a pure-blooded negro of the brown or semi-copper-colored variety. He was without a trace of beard, as that variety of negro usually is. His voice was a falsetto.

His devotion was dog-like. If the state of South Carolina held anything that his mess needed, and there was any conceivable way in which it could be got, he got it. Frankly without morals, — unless devotion to his mess was a moral sentiment, — and illimitable in resource as he was, he generally so managed matters that we should live well.

We would buy a pig or a lamb, and have a fore quarter for dinner. The next day Curry would give us a hind quarter. The next day another fore quarter; and so on until that member of the mess who had a statistical mind would begin to reflect that there are really only four quarters to an animal, while we had had from fifteen to twenty quarters from this one. Then Curry would be summoned, and indignantly asked: "Where have you been getting all this meat we have been eating?"

The question never disturbed Curry in the least. He was always ready with the answer: "I buyed it from one man, sir."

When asked who the man was, he never knew. And when questioned as to payment, he always assured us that the "one man, sir," was coming that afternoon for his money.

The "one man, sir," always came that afternoon. His charge was always the same: $2.50 in Confederate currency, or something less than twenty-five cents in real money.

The pretence was a bit flimsy, but it answered Curry's purpose. His mess was well fed, and he was not caught in his raids upon the pig-pens and sheep-folds thereabouts.

Curry was a slave, and we hired him from the estate to which he belonged as a chattel. One day we were ordered to move from South Carolina to Virginia. Curry came to us and asked to be taken with us. When we explained to him that we could not legally take him out of the state, he deliberately proposed to run away in order to go with us. Having no alert perception of the difference between crime and good conduct, he could not see why we should not abet him in this proposed violation of law. But when we made it clear to him that, for reasons inscrutable to his mind, we could not permit him to go with us out of the state, he fell into melancholy.

That night we had some roast pig for dinner; and Curry had not "buyed it from one man, sir."

The only reply he would make to our questionings was: "I done got it fur de mess, sir. De mess has been good to me."

Early next morning — the day on which we were to leave — the enemy landed below, and we were ordered forward to meet them. As we unlimbered in battery and opened fire, Curry rode up on an antique mule, stolen for the occasion from the battery blacksmith. Leaping from his steed he went to the gun that was most shorthanded, took a vacant place, and began fighting like an artilleryman. When the head of the mess rode up to him and said: "What are you doing here, Curry?"

His reply was: "Ise takin' a hand."

The fight was hot for ten minutes. At the end of it poor Curry lay stretched upon the grass — a bullet through his chest. One of us went to him and said something — no matter what. He looked up and said : " I can't go wi' de mess to Virginy. You'll have to take some no 'count nigger. But Ise fought wi' de mess anyhow, and you'll find de res' o' dat pig hangin' up de chimbly."

GUN-BOATS

A GUN-BOAT went aground one night in an inlet off Chisholm's Island, near Port Royal, South Carolina.

As soon as the news came to us, we set out to attack her.

We marched all night, and in the early gray of the dawn we reached the palmetto-studded island. The gun-boat had, in the meantime, got off the bar on the high tide, and was riding quietly at anchor, four hundred yards from the nearest available point on the shore.

I had command of two field pieces. Captain Elliot, the chief of artillery, ordered me to inspect the vessel and "act according to circumstances." He said: "If you find her too strong to be attacked with field guns, retire quietly across the island. If you find her not too strong, attack her, and I will send you any reinforcements necessary."

I took Joe with me.

We crawled up to the brink of the stream, and took a good look in the gray morning light.

But that look didn't tell either of us anything. Neither of us knew enough about naval architecture and armament to have the slightest idea whether the boat out there in the stream was formidable or otherwise.

"Well, what do you think, Joe?" I asked. "I don't think," he answered; "I don't know anything about it; but my notion is that we'd better give her a shot or two, anyhow."

"Well, the way I look at it," said I, "is this: Elliot and those other fellows know, and we don't. They'll see her from some point of view. If they think her not formidable, and we don't attack, they'll blame us. If we attack, and she proves too formidable — well, we've got good horses and we can run. Order up the guns, Joe."

A minute later we opened fire with two twelve pounders. By one of those freaks of extraordinarily good luck, which so often save men from disaster in war, our first shot severed the gunboat's rudder post. Our second shell passed through her boiler and exploded in her furnace; not only setting fire to her, but with the escaping steam driving the men from the gun decks. This left her with only one available gun — a swivel on the poop.

But that was a sixty-four pound howitzer, one or two shots from which would have swept us off that island like so much dust. Our good luck continuing, however, that gun burst at the first fire.

The ship had been a formidable, heavily armed gun-boat, carrying several eight-inch rifles; but she had been destroyed by two field pop-guns. She slipped her cables, and drifted around the point with fire bursting from every port hole. We quickly limbered up and galloped to another point of attack.

We found the ship's company escaping over the sides in the boats and rowing for the marsh beyond. We opened upon them at short range, sank several of the boats, and then shelled the marsh for scatterers.

When I learned later from Captain Elliot how formidable that ship had been, I was filled with a great contempt for gun-boats. I was anxious to get a chance at a gun-boat every morning before breakfast.

I got it presently. With that same section I was ordered a few days later to Combahee Ferry. There was a gun-boat there. My orders were the same as before.

This gun-boat was a little, low, insignificant looking sloop. She seemed to me almost contemptibly easy game. I galloped my guns to within four hundred yards of her, and ordered them in battery.

We opened fire. The gun-boat for a time paid no attention to us. But by the time that we had thrown three or four shells at her, she lazily undertook to attend to our case, in much the same way that a man brushes a pestilent fly from his nose.

She opened on us with one of those great guns which pitch shells about the size of a normal nail keg two or three miles, apparently without effort.

Her first shot revealed to me the fact that I had entirely misunderstood gun-boats.

It was obvious that a single one of those shells, should it burst anywhere in the neighborhood of my guns, would put a final end to that section of artillery and to all that went to constitute it.

During the next five minutes we bumped those guns at a gallop over the old cotton rows, until we reached the cover of the woodland.

Whether that little sloop carried one gun or twenty, I never knew. But the rapidity of her fire, as we crossed that old cotton field, convinced me, for the time being, that she carried at least a hundred.

TWO MINUTES

HE spent the evening singing "Lorena." He had had a sort of day-off that day, and had visited all of his friends.

The author of that song had made it read: —

"A hundred weeks have passed, Lorena,"

but our guest improved upon that, and made the lover rather aged by singing it: —

"A hundred *years* have passed, Lorena,
Since last I held thy hand in mine."

This was the only positive evidence we had that he had been calling.

He stayed with us that night, and was not feeling well enough the next day even to sing "Lorena." The next day after that he found some serious work to do.

The way of it was this: He was a third lieutenant in the engineers. It was after the great mine explosion at Petersburg, and the engineers were busily engaged at that time using all their devices for the discovery of other mines. They had found one in process of construction in front of General Gracie's lines. They had proceeded at once to run a deeper tunnel under this one. They had loaded the end of it, just underneath the enemy's works, with an incredible amount of gunpowder, and on that morning it was to be fired.

A slow-match had been brought from the powder to the mouth of the mine. It was lighted, and a period of waiting ensued. The match had evidently gone out. Where, nobody knew or could guess. The general in command of that part of the line turned to the captain of engineers and said: "The mine must be blown up at once; will you go in and light the match again?"

The captain hesitated, saying: "I don't know; it may go off at any moment."

Thereupon he who had sung "Lorena" stepped forward, touched his cap to the general, and said: "With your permission, *I* will go in and fire it."

"Thank you," said the general; "go."

The man picked up the torch and started into the mine. It seems that the slow-match had gone out within a very short distance of the powder magazine. But disregarding that he touched the torch to it, set it off again, and ran with all his might for the mouth of the opening.

It was two minutes' work. The mine went off just before he reached the outlet, and the air pressure literally blew him out of it. He fell sprawling on his face. He was considerably bruised and scratched in his contact with the gravelly ground, but he was not in any serious way injured. Picking himself up, grimed as he was, he took off his cap, and dusting himself like a schoolboy who has fallen in the street, he approached the commanding officer and said: "General, I have the honor to report that I have fired the mine and that it has gone off."

The general touched his cap and replied: "I had observed that fact, and I thank you very much. I beg to say that I will make an official report of the circumstance."

Two days later we all touched our caps to a freshly made brigadier-general of the engineers. The captain who had hesitated remained a captain.

SI TUCKER—COWARD AND HERO

I WAS in command of Fort Lamkin, a mortar fort, in rear of General Bushrod Johnson's lines at Petersburg in 1864.

The fort was named for our immediate commander, from whose command we had been detached for this service.

One day Lamkin himself came to me when I was at his headquarters. He was obviously in trouble.

"This boy, Si Tucker," he said, "is the son of one of the best friends I ever had in the world. The boy is a coward. He literally *lives* in a rat hole. I have repeatedly pulled him out by the legs, only to have him crawl back again the moment I let go of his ankles. I don't know what to do. It's my duty, of course, to prefer charges of cowardice against him; and if I do, he will certainly be shot — and his father is my best friend."

He paused meditatively, and then said with eagerness in his voice: "Why can't you take him?"

I agreed at once. I told him I would take

the boy with me to my pits, and make "either a soldier or a stiff" out of him within the next twenty-four hours. I was under no obligations to his father; I had never even met any of his relatives, and I had seen too many years of service to have much patience with cowardice.

The boy was sent for and ordered to go with me. We walked down towards Blandford church. At the proper point we turned out of the Jerusalem plank road across the fields towards Fort Lamkin. Half-way there and on the top of a little hill, which was especially exposed to the gaze of the sharp-shooters, I made Si Tucker sit down by my side. There we came to an understanding.

I told him that he had been assigned to me to be shot out of hand, or to be court-martialled for cowardice, which at that particular juncture of the war meant very much the same thing. I explained to him that he was about to join a detachment, composed exclusively of men specially selected for their courage — every one of them a volunteer for what was deemed a peculiarly dangerous service.

I explained further that I should require him to do his duty as they did theirs.

"You have managed to make for yourself," I said, "the reputation of a coward. You have now one last chance to redeem yourself. You must do that, or you must die."

The sharp-shooters were, in the meantime, picking at us most uncomfortably as we sat there. My experience as an old soldier strongly suggested to me that we ought to move. The position was of that kind that military men call untenable. Nevertheless, I thought it best to keep Si Tucker there a minute longer, for purposes of observation, if nothing else.

"At our pits," I said, "we have one uniform rule of procedure. When a bombardment begins, the men go to their guns. I take my stand on top of the magazine mound to watch the enemy's fire and direct our own. If I see that a mortar shell is about to fall into one of the gun pits, I call out the pit number, and the men run into the bomb-proof until the explosion is over. No man ever goes into a bomb-proof till this order is given. You must do as the rest do. If you run to a bomb-proof before I have given the order, it will be my imperative duty to shoot you then and there; and I shall certainly discharge that duty. Do you fully understand that, Si?"

He thought he did, and as the sharp-shooters were by this time becoming pestilently personal in their attentions, we resumed our walk.

Half an hour after our arrival at Fort Lamkin, a bombardment began.

I didn't want to shoot that boy. I distinctly preferred to make a soldier rather than a "stiff" out of him. So, instead of taking my customary stand on the mound of earth over the magazine, I ordered Joe to that post, and placed myself in the gun pit to which Si Tucker had been assigned, taking care to stand between him and the mouth of the bomb-proof. I spoke to him as I passed.

"Remember what I told you. If you forget, it is instant death."

He remembered. For nearly two hours he stood there quaking and quivering, but not daring to seek safety by retreat to a bomb-proof.

By the time that the outburst was over, Si Tucker had learned his first lesson in war. He had learned to realize that a man may endure a lot of very savage fire, and yet come out of it alive.

A few hours later, when the guns were at work again, Si was steady enough in his nerves to carry shells to the guns. The next day he was even able during a bombardment to cut fuses — a delicate operation requiring a steady hand.

Within two or three days he had become as good a soldier as we had in all that band of men specially picked for their unflinching courage.

When the great mine explosion occurred a few weeks later, I had occasion to rebuke Si Tucker for a fault quite unrelated to cowardice. We had been ordered to go with our mortars as near as possible to the crater, and to drop a continual rain of shells among the thousands of helpless fellows in that awful pit.

It was cruel, ghastly work. But it was war. And a poet has justly characterized war as a "brain-spattering, windpipe-slitting art." Or as General Sherman once said, — and he knew, — "War is all hell."

We were within sixty yards of the crater. Each one of our mortars was belching from three to five shells a minute into that hole; but Si Tucker's enthusiasm was not satisfied. Having no personal duty to do at the moment, he began plugging shells with long fuses, lighting them, running with them to the margin of the pit, and tossing them in as hand grenades. He was greeted by a tremendous volley of musketry at each repetition of this performance, but he did it three times before we could stop him.

That evening, near the gloaming, he did another thing. The lines had by that time been restored. The men in the crater — those of them who had not been killed — had been driven back to the Federal side. We became aware of the fact that a poor fellow of our own was lying grievously wounded near the Federal side of the fifty yards that separated our works from the enemy's. He had been lying there through all that long, fierce summer day. The explosion at daylight had cast him there.

His groans and his cries for help and for water were piteous in the extreme. We listened to them heartbroken but helpless — all but Si Tucker.

Si began stripping off his clothes; we thought he had gone mad. But when we asked him why he was stripping himself, he replied: "Never you mind."

With that, stripped to the skin, he leaped over the works, ducked his head low, and ran through that hailstorm of bullets to where the wounded man lay. Grasping him quickly, he slung him upon his back like a bag of meal, and ran back with all his might.

As he crossed the works he fell headlong.

The surgeon found three bullets in his body.

Nobody in the battery ever remembered after that, that Si Tucker had once been a coward.

After all, it is perhaps mainly a question of nerves.

WAR AS A THERAPEUTIC AGENT

DOCTOR TOWNS was a wealthy gentleman in Mississippi.

For a good many years he had employed Miss R—— of Massachusetts as governess for his daughters. She had lived all these years as an honored member of his family, with every social opportunity that Mississippi society afforded.

At last the two girls outgrew the need of a governess. One of them was sent abroad to study art at Nuremberg. The other got married.

Upon the occurrence of this event Doctor Towns went to the young lady, Miss R——, and suggested that as her services had been of incalculable value to his daughters he was anxious to secure for her, now that they no longer needed her, an equally good situation in some other gentleman's family.

He explained that he had already written to a friend in Alabama strongly recommending her, and that his friend desired her to come on at once.

Apparently this pleased Miss R—— very greatly. She packed her trunks that night with the aid of the colored maid who had been assigned to her service. She was to leave in the morning.

In the morning word came down from her chamber that she was unable to get up. Every attention and every sympathy was shown her, and after a day or two Doctor Towns, finding himself baffled to discover disease of any kind, sent for another physician. The other physician was equally unsuccessful. The simple fact was that the young woman could not get out of her bed. Why she could not get out of her bed was a problem that the medical men were wholly unable to solve. The young woman's appetite was excellent, and all her functions seemed to be in an entirely normal condition.

Nevertheless, she could not get up.

Week after week she lay there, attentively waited upon by the servants, assiduously visited by the family, sympathetically condoled with by friends, but still utterly unable to arise from her bed. Her salary was continued all the while, of course.

The servants at last became suspicious.

To their minds it seemed incredible that she should live so long and so comfortably without exercise. They suspected that she got up in the night and walked the floor. To test this they gently sprinkled her floor with pulverized starch while she slept, and then turned out the lights. But weeks of experimentation of this character utterly failed to reveal that the young woman ever got out of her bed.

She read the newspapers with great diligence every day, and she read all the new books that came out, for they all came to Doctor Towns's household.

She even wrote now and then, lying there in bed, for newspapers and magazines with which she had established connections. She was a brilliant woman, and her matter was acceptable in the market.

She lay thus, for eighteen months. Then came secession.

The newspapers were filled with it. When at last war became an obvious fact, and escape from the South to any Northern person disinclined to Southern policies was manifestly a matter of but a few days, Miss R—— suddenly, I may almost say miraculously, recovered. She got up one morning and packed her trunks before six o'clock. At seven, when the family breakfast was served, she appeared in the dining-room, and calmly asked: "Will you kindly send me to the railroad station, Doctor Towns? I'm going North to-day."

No explanation was ever asked or ever given.

Miss R—— went North. That was all.

"NOTES ON COLD HARBOR"[1]

I ALWAYS think of our arrival at Cold Harbor as marking a new phase of the war.

By the time that we had reached that position, we had pretty well got over our astonishment and disappointment at the conduct of General Grant.

I put the matter in that way because, as I remember, astonishment and disappointment were the prevailing emotions in the ranks of the army of Northern Virginia when we discovered, after the contest in the Wilderness, that General Grant was not going to retire behind the river and permit General Lee to carry on a campaign against Washington in the usual way, but was moving to the Spottsylvania position instead.

We had been accustomed to a program which began with a Federal advance, culminated in one great battle, and ended in the retirement of the Union army, the substitution of a new Federal commander for the one beaten, and the

---

[1] These notes were originally printed in the great war book of the Century Company, entitled: "Battles and Leaders of the Civil War." They are here reprinted by the courteous and very generous permission of the Century Company.

institution of a more or less offensive campaign on our part.

This was the usual order of events, and this was what we confidently expected when General Grant crossed into the Wilderness. But here was a new Federal general, fresh from the West, and so ill informed as to the military customs in our part of the country, that when the battle of the Wilderness was over, instead of retiring to the north bank of the river, and awaiting the development of Lee's plans, he had the temerity to move by his left flank to a new position, there to try conclusions with us again.

We were greatly disappointed with General Grant, and full of curiosity to know how long it was going to take him to perceive the impropriety of his course.

But by the time that we reached Cold Harbor, we had begun to understand what our new adversary meant, and there, for the first time I think, the men in the ranks of the army of Northern Virginia realized that the era of experimental campaigns against us was over; that Grant was not going to retreat; that he was not to be removed from command because he had failed to break Lee's resistance; and that the policy of pounding had begun, and would continue until our strength should be utterly worn away, unless by some decisive blow to the army in our front, or some brilliant movement in diversion,— such as Early's invasion of Maryland a little later was intended to be,— we should succeed in changing the character of the contest.

We began to understand that Grant had taken hold of the problem of destroying the Confederate strength in the only way that the strength of such an army, so commanded, could be destroyed, and that he intended to continue the plodding work till the task should be accomplished, wasting very little time or strength in efforts to make a brilliant display of generalship in a contest of strategic wits with Lee. We at last began to understand what Grant had meant by his expression of a determination to "fight it out on this line, if it takes all summer."

Our state of mind, however, was curiously illustrative of the character of the contest, and of the people who participated in it on the part of the South. The Southern folk were always debaters, loving logic, and taking off their hats to a syllogism.

They had never been able to understand how any reasonable mind could doubt the right of secession, or fail to see the unlawfulness and iniquity of coercion, and they were in a chronic state of astonished incredulity, as the war began, that the North could indeed be about to wage a war that was manifestly forbidden by unimpeachable logic.

In the same way, at Cold Harbor, we were all disposed to waste a good deal of intellectual energy in demonstrating to each other the absurd and unreasonable character of General Grant's procedure. We could show that he must have lost already in that campaign more men than Lee's entire force, and ought, logically, to acknowledge his defeat and retire; that having begun the contest with an overwhelming advantage in point of numbers, he ought to be ashamed to ask for reinforcements; and that while continuing the process of suffering great losses, in order to inflict much smaller losses on us, he could ultimately wear us out, it was inconceivable that any general should consent to win in that unfair way.

In like manner we were prepared to prove the wicked imbecility of his plan of campaign — a plan that could only end by placing him in a position below Richmond and Petersburg, which he might just as well reach by an advance from Fort Monroe, without the tremendous slaughter of the Wilderness, Spottsylvania, etc.

In view of General Grant's stolid indifference to considerations of this character, however, there was nothing for us to do but fight the matter out.

We had no fear of the ultimate result, however plainly our own perception of facts pointed to the inevitable destruction of our power of resistance. We had absolute faith in Lee's ability to meet and repel any assault that might be made, and to devise some means of destroying Grant. There was, therefore, no fear in the Confederate ranks of anything that General Grant might do; but there was an appalling and well-founded fear of starvation, which indeed some of us were already suffering. From the beginning of that campaign our food-supply had been barely sufficient to maintain life, and on the march from Spottsylvania to Cold Harbor it would have been a gross exaggeration to describe it in that way.

In my own battery, three hard biscuits and one very meagre slice of fat pork were issued to each man on our arrival, and that was the first food that any of us had seen since our departure from Spottsylvania, two days before. The next supply did not come till two days later, and it consisted of a single cracker per man, with no meat at all.

We practised a very rigid economy with this food, of course. We ate the pork raw, partly because there was no convenient means of cooking it, but more because cooking would have involved some waste. We hoarded what we had, allowing ourselves only a nibble at any one time, and that only when the pangs of hunger became unbearable.

But what is the use of writing about the pangs of hunger? The words arc utterly meaningless to persons who have never known actual starvation, and they cannot be made other than meaningless. Hunger to starving men is wholly unrelated to the desire for food as that is commonly understood and felt. It is a great agony of the whole body and soul as well. It is an unimaginable, all-pervading pain, inflicted when the strength to endure pain is utterly gone. It is the great, despairing cry of a wasting body — a cry of flesh and blood, marrow, nerves, bones, and faculties for strength with which to exist and to endure existence. It is a horror which, once suffered, leaves an impression that is never erased from the memory, and to this day the agony of that campaign comes back upon me at the mere thought of any living creature's lacking the food it desires, even though its hunger be only the ordinary craving, and the denial be necessary for the creature's health.

When we reached Cold Harbor, the command to which I belonged had been marching almost continuously day and night for more than fifty hours without food; and, for the first time, we knew what actual starvation was. It was during that march that I heard a man wish himself a woman, — the only case of the kind I ever heard of, — and he uttered the wish half in grim jest, and made haste to qualify it by adding "or a baby."

Yet we recovered our cheerfulness at once after taking the first nibble of the crackers issued to us there, and made a jest of the scantiness of the supply. One tall, lean mountaineer, Jim Thomas by name, who received a slight wound every time he was under fire, and was never sufficiently hurt to quit duty, was standing on a bank of earth slowly munching a bit of his last cracker and watching the effect of some artillery fire which was in progress at the time, when a bullet carried away his cap and cut a strip of hair from his head, leaving the scalp for a space as bald as if it had been shaved with a razor. He sat down at once to nurse a sharp headache, and then discovered that the cracker he had held in his hand was gone, leaving a mere fragment in his grasp. At first he was in doubt whether he might not have eaten it unconsciously; but he quickly discovered that it had been knocked out of his hand and crushed to bits by a bullet, whereupon as he sat there in an exposed place, where the fire was unobstructed, he lamented his loss in soliloquy.

"If I had eaten that cracker half an hour ago, it would have been safe," he said. "I should have had none left for next time, but I have none left as it is. That shows how foolish it is to save anything. Whew! how my head aches. I wish it was from overeating, but even the doctor couldn't lay it to that just now. The next time I stand up to watch the firing, I'll put my cracker — if I have any — in a safe place down by the breastworks, where it won't get wounded, poor thing! By the way, here's a little piece left, and that'll get shot while I sit here talking." And with that he jumped down into the ditch, carefully placed the mouthful of hardtack at the foot of the works, and resumed his interested observation of the artillery duel.

Trifling of that kind was constant among the men throughout that terrible campaign from the Wilderness to Petersburg, and while it yielded nothing worth recording as wit or humor, it has always seemed to me the most remarkable and most significant fact in the history of the time. It revealed a capacity for cheerful endurance which alone made the campaign possible on the Confederate side.

With mercenary troops or regulars the resistance that Lee was able to offer to Grant's tremendous pressure would have been impossible in such circumstances. The starvation and the excessive marching would have destroyed the morale of troops held together only by discipline. No historical criticism of our Civil War can be otherwise than misleading if it omits to

"Notes on Cold Harbor"

give a prominent place, as a factor, to the character of the volunteers on both sides, who, in acquiring the steadiness and order of regulars, never lost their personal interest in the contest, or their personal pride of manhood as a sustaining force under trying conditions. If either side had lacked this element of personal heroism on the part of its men, it would have been driven from the field long before 1865. It seems to me the most important duty of those who now furnish the materials out of which the ultimate history of our Civil War will be constructed to emphasize this aspect of the matter, and in every possible way to illustrate the part which the high personal character of the volunteers in the ranks played in determining the events of the contest. For that reason I like to record one incident which I had an opportunity to observe at Cold Harbor.

Immediately opposite the position occupied by the battery to which I belonged, and about six or eight hundred yards distant across an open field, lay a Federal battery, whose commander was manifestly a man deeply in earnest for other and higher reasons than those that govern the professional soldier: a man who fought well, because he fought in what he felt to be his own cause and quarrel.

His guns and ours were engaged almost continuously in an artillery duel, so that I became especially interested in him, particularly as the extreme precision of his fire indicated thoroughness and conscientiousness of work for months before the campaign began. One day — whether before or after the great assault, I cannot now remember — that part of our line which lay immediately to the left of the position occupied by the battery to which I belonged was thrown forward to force the opposing Federal line back. It was the only large movement in the way of a charge over perfectly open ground that I ever had a chance to observe with an unobstructed view, and merely as a spectator.

When we, with a few well-aimed shells, had fired a barn that stood between the lines, and driven a multitude of sharp-shooters out of it, the troops to our left leaped over our works and with a cheer moved rapidly across the field. The resistance made to their advance was not very determined, — probably the Federal line at that point had been weakened by concentration elsewhere, — and after a brief struggle our men crossed the slight Federal earthworks and pressed their adversaries back into the woods and beyond my view. It was a beautiful operation to look at, and one, the like of which, a soldier rarely has an opportunity to see so well; but my attention was specially drawn to the situation of the artillery commander, to whom I have referred as posted immediately in our front. His position was the pivot, the point where the Federal line was broken to a new angle, when that part of it which lay upon his right hand was pressed back while that on his left remained stationary.

He fought like a Turk or a tiger.

He directed the greater part of his fire upon the advancing line of Confederates, but turned a gun every few minutes upon our battery, apparently by way of letting us know that he was not unmindful of our attentions, even when he was so busily engaged elsewhere.

The bending back of the line on his right presently subjected him to a murderous fire upon the flank and rear,—a fire against which he had no protection whatever,—while we continued a furious bombardment from the front. His position was plainly an untenable one, and so far as I could discover with a strong glass, he was for a time without infantry support. But he held his ground and continued to fight in spite of all, firing at one time as from two faces of an acute triangle.

His determination was superb, and the coolness of his gunners and cannoneers was worthy of the unbounded admiration which we, their enemies, felt for them. Their firing increased as their difficulties multiplied, but it showed no sign of becoming wild or hurried. Every shot went straight to the object against which it was directed; every fuse was accurately timed, and every shell burst where it was intended to burst. I remember that in the very heat of the contest there came into my mind Bulwer's superb description of Warwick's last struggle, in which he says that around the king-maker's person there "centred a little WAR," and I applied the phrase to the heroic fellow who was so superbly fighting against hopeless odds immediately in front of me.

Several of his guns were dismounted and his dead horses were strewn in the rear. The loss among his men was appalling, but he fought on as coolly as before, and with our glasses we could see him calmly sitting on his large gray horse directing his gunners and patiently awaiting the coming of the infantry support, without which he could not withdraw his guns. It came at last, and the batteries retired to the new line.

When the battalion was gone and the brief action over, the wreck that was left behind bore sufficient witness of the fearfulness of the fire so coolly endured. The large gray horse lay dead upon the ground; but we preferred to believe that his brave rider was still alive to receive the promotion which he had so well won.

A PLANTATION HEROINE

It was nearing the end.

Every resource of the Southern states had been taxed to the point of exhaustion.

The people had given up everything they had for "the cause."

Under the law of a "tax in kind," they had surrendered all they could spare of food products of every character. Under an untamable impulse of patriotism they had surrendered much more than they could spare in order to feed the army.

It was at such a time that I went to my home county on a little military business. I stopped for dinner at a house, the lavish hospitality of which had been a byword in the old days.

I found before me at dinner the remnants of a cold boiled ham, some boiled mustard greens, which we Virginians called "salad," a pitcher of butter-milk, some corn-pones and — nothing else.

I carved the ham, and offered to serve it to the three women of the household. But they all declined. They made their dinner on salad, butter-milk, and corn-bread, the latter eaten very sparingly, as I observed. The ham went only to myself and to the three convalescent wounded soldiers, who were guests in the house.

Wounded men were at that time guests in every house in Virginia.

I lay awake that night and thought over the circumstance. The next morning I took occasion to have a talk on the old familiar terms with the young woman of the family, with whom I had been on a basis of friendship in the old days that even permitted me to kiss her upon due and proper occasion.

"Why didn't you take some ham last night?" I asked urgently.

"Oh, I didn't want it," she replied.

"Now, you know you're fibbing," I said. "Tell me the truth, won't you?"

She blushed, and hesitated. Presently she broke down and answered frankly: "Honestly, I did want the ham. I have hungered for meat for months. But I mustn't eat it, and I won't. You see the army needs all the food there is, and more. We women can't fight, though I don't see at all why they shouldn't let us, and so we are trying to feed the fighting men — and there aren't any others. We've made up our minds not to eat anything that can be sent to the front as rations."

"You are starving yourselves," I exclaimed.

"Oh, no," she said. "And if we were, what would it matter? Haven't Lee's soldiers starved many a day? But we aren't starving. You see we had plenty of salad and butter-milk last night. And we even ate some of the cornbread. I must stop that, by the way, for corn-meal is a good ration for the soldiers."

A month or so later this frail but heroic young girl was laid away in the Grub Hill church-yard.

Don't talk to me about the "heroism" that braves a fire of hell under enthusiastic impulse. That young girl did a higher act of self-sacrifice than any soldier who fought on either side during the war ever dreamed of doing.

TWO INCIDENTS IN CONTRAST

INCIDENT NUMBER ONE

THE Masters place at Amelia Court House was a dream of beauty. Major Masters himself was a man of exquisite taste, and his wife and daughter had been devoted for years to the creation of beauty there.

They had had the expert aid of Thomas Giles. Thomas Giles was a lawyer by profession, but being a man of large wealth, and having nobody dependent upon him, he had devoted a considerable share of his attention for years to his two fancies — architecture and landscape gardening.

It had been his long-continued custom to spend his time from Friday afternoon till Monday of each week at the Masters place, developing its possibilities of beauty. He had spent both his own money and that of Major Masters very lavishly in this endeavor, and the result was a notable one.

When the Federal army reached the court house in hot pursuit of General Lee, during that last retreat which ended the war, there was a rush made by the soldiers for comfortable camping grounds on the Masters place. One man had even begun to cut down a stately tree for firewood, when the general commanding rode up. Taking in the situation at a glance, the general turned to one of his aids and said: "Take a squad of twenty men, and drive everybody out of that place quick. Then tell the adjutant-general to post a close guard around it and allow no man to enter it during our stay, upon any pretence whatever."

Then, turning to his staff as the officer rode away to execute his orders, he said: "That place has cost years of growth as well as years of intelligent endeavor to create it. As we are not vandals, I shall not suffer it to be destroyed."

I regret that I cannot here record the name of that officer. I would if I knew it.

INCIDENT NUMBER TWO

At McPhersonville, on the coast of South Carolina, there lived a young woman of extraordinary learning.

The fame of her learning, especially in botany, had even crossed the ocean; and it was she whom Baron Von Humboldt had selected to prepare for him — for use in his writings — an account of the flora of that region.

In recognition of her scholarly service, Baron Von Humboldt had sent to her — each volume inscribed with his own hand — the only copy ever owned in the United States of the German government's magnificent édition de luxe of "Cosmos."

It was a work published without regard to expense, and in narrowly limited edition, at a fabulous price per copy.

When the final collapse came, and Sherman's army was sweeping northward from Savannah, a detachment under the command of a lieutenant visited the house of this young woman. Building a bonfire in the front yard, it proceeded to destroy all the food that it could find. Then, in a spirit of pure vandalism, the lieutenant ordered his men to bring out and burn the books in that superb library. The young woman was in tears and terror, of course, but her scholarly impulses rose superior to her timid, feminine instincts. She went up to the lieutenant, coarse brute that he was, and begged for the preservation of her unique "Cosmos."

She explained to him what it was and how much it meant to scholarship. She begged him to take it with him and present it to Yale, or Harvard, or Princeton, or to the Astor library, or to any other institution of learning to which it might become a possession of glory.

He slapped her in the face, and with his own hands threw the precious volumes into the fire.

A nation at war must select its human instruments with regard to their capacity for fighting, and with very little regard to anything else. Whether the officer be a gentleman or a blackguard is a matter that counts for little so long as he knows how to fight.

But I regret that I cannot here record the name of *this* officer also.

HOW THE SERGEANT-MAJOR TOLD THE TRUTH

SO far as I know, the sergeant-major never told a lie in his life; but he came very near it that night at Grahamville.

Grahamville is a village on the Charleston and Savannah railroad, and this was in 1862, when the enemy held the sea islands along that coast. Whenever they landed and advanced toward the railroad, it was our business to march down and meet them at such points of vantage as the marshes and causeways afforded.

The battery had been stationed at Grahamville about two months, and, as the enemy had been inactive all that time, there was nothing whatever to do; nothing, that is to say, except to practise with pistols on the bullet-proof hide of an antique alligator, which used to lie upon a log in the swamp in front of us sunning himself and apparently rather enjoying the impingement of bullets upon his ribs. We had pretty well exhausted that amusement; so when the news came that there was to be a dance at Tucker's, — about twelve miles in rear of

Grahamville, — the captain, the one lieutenant on duty, and the surgeon promptly accepted the invitation. They omitted the formality of sending to headquarters for leave of absence. They simply went.

The sergeant-major, who carried on a voluminous correspondence with various young women in different parts of the Confederacy, had letters to write and preferred to remain behind. Besides that, his boots were broken out on both sides, and his linen coat — the only thing he had that was cool enough for such an occasion in such a climate — had only one button on it, and that one a black one sewed on with white thread. The sergeant-major rather valued himself upon his personal pulchritude, and preferred solitude in the camp to any unfavorable exhibition of himself and his wardrobe. So the sergeant-major was left in command of the battery.

It was on that particular night, of course, that the enemy concluded to make a threatening landing on the coast below. Hurried orders came from General Clingman for the battery to move forward at once. The sergeant-major received the orders, had the assembly blown, and promptly moved forward with the guns. He was a very earnest and conscientious young man. That is why he came so near telling lies that night. He was fond of his officers and very much devoted to their welfare. It would have gone hard with them had their absence become known to the commanding general.

As the sergeant-major rode along in the murkiness of a cloudy, Southern midnight at the head of the battery, General Clingman rode up and asked, "Where's your captain?"

"He's in rear," said the sergeant-major. Now, strictly speaking, this was the exact truth. The captain was in rear — twelve or fifteen miles in rear! Nevertheless the sergeant-major felt an uncomfortable consciousness that his words conveyed to the mind of the general an impression that was not quite accurate. When the general inquired about the one other officer supposed to be on duty at that time, the sergeant-major replied: "He also is somewhere in rear at the moment." You see the sergeant-major was getting used to this sort of thing.

The general replied; "Well, it's no matter, you can take the orders and communicate them."

Thereupon he gave instructions as to the disposition of the guns in case of a fight. After that he rode to the front. It was his habit to be at the front as his force approached an enemy.

An hour or two later our returning cavalry reported that the enemy had returned to his island camp. Our long night march had gone for nothing. We were a little bit disappointed, but as we had marched during all the hours of darkness, and as the gray was beginning to split the eastern sky, we were not very reluctant to turn back towards camp and breakfast.

But when, soon after the return march began, the sergeant-major saw the general riding up, he felt a trifle uneasy. You see he was not yet an artist in prevarication. His life-long habit of telling the truth sat heavily upon him. Nevertheless, when the general asked for the captain and lieutenant, the sergeant-major said, with as much of nonchalance as he could assume: "They're somewhere in *front*, I think, general," and the general rode away satisfied. When the battery reached camp, the officers had just returned from the dance at Tucker's. They were frantic with apprehension and rage at finding their command gone to fight the enemy and they not with it. They were minutely questioning the camp servants as to the movement. And when the sergeant-major rode up at the head of the column of guns, they assailed him with a volley of questions, which, if they had been shells, would have struck the enemy off any field: the sergeant-major rather enjoyed this part of the proceeding.

"What kind of a time did you have at Tucker's?" he asked.

"Oh, confound Tucker's!" answered the captain. "Speak, can't you, man, and tell us about this thing. Did the general ask after us, and what did you tell him?"

"Well," answered the sergeant-major, "he did ask, and I told him the truth, but not the whole truth. My conscience is a little bit bruised and sore over it, and the next time you fellows go off to a dance without letting the general know, I'm going to tell him the whole truth. Is there anything to eat?"

TWO GENTLEMEN AT PETERSBURG

AT that point where the great mine was blown up at Petersburg, the lines of the two armies were within fifty yards of each other.

In the fearful slaughter that ensued, the space between the rival breastworks was literally piled high with dead men, lying one on top of the other. Only in one other place, namely, at Cold Harbor, was there ever so much of slaughter within so small a space.

It was evident, apart from all considerations of decency, that for the comfort of both sides some arrangement must be made for the burial of these dead men. Neither side could have lived long in its works otherwise.

Accordingly, a cartel was arranged between General Grant and General Lee. It was stipulated that there should be a cessation of hostilities for a specified number of hours for the purpose of burying the dead.

It was arranged that two lines should be formed twelve feet apart in the middle of the space between the works; that one line should be composed of Federal sentinels, the other of Confederates; that the space between these two lines should be a neutral ground, accessible to both sides; but that no person from either side should cross the line established by the other side. It was agreed that the dead men who had fallen within the Confederate line should be dragged to the neutral ground by Confederate soldiers, and there delivered to Federal troops to be carried within their lines for burial.

There were no Confederate dead there, of course. All of our men who had been killed were killed within our own works. So every corpse on our side of the neutral ground was dragged by a rope to that common space and there delivered to its official friends.

It was specially stipulated in the cartel that no officer or soldier on either side should take advantage of the truce to appropriate property of any kind lying upon the field, whether upon the one or the other side of the neutral ground. Swords, pistols, sashes, everything of the kind must, by agreement, be left precisely where they were.

Many of us, of course, went out to the neutral ground to look over the situation. There was a certain gruesome delight even in standing upon ground, where for a month or more it had been impossible for a twig or a blade of grass to grow without instant decapitation, and where for months to come it would be equally impossible for anything having material substance to exist. The very turf itself had been literally skinned from the surface of the earth by a continuous scything of bullets. For a month it had been impossible for any soldier on either side even to shoot over the breastworks, for he who tried to do so was sure to be instantly destroyed. The fire on either side had to be through carefully sand-bag-guarded port holes. And even the port holes had to be protected by hanging blankets behind them to conceal the sky, lest their darkening by a human head should invite a hailstorm of alert and waiting bullets.

Of course every man who, during the truce, wandered over this perilous space for an hour, must have been impressed, if he had any imagination at all, with the historical interest of the occasion. Every one desired naturally to carry away some memento of the event. Only one man yielded to this impulse, and he did so thoughtlessly. He was a captain of Confederate infantry.

He saw lying on the ground a star that had been cut by a bullet from some officer's coat collar.

It was a worthless bauble, valuable only as a souvenir. He picked it up and pocketed it. Instantly he was arrested by the Confederate guards and taken before the officer in command of the Confederate line.

That officer immediately and with great dignity went to the Federal commander and said: "I desire under the terms of the cartel to surrender this officer to you for such punishment as a court-martial of your army may see fit to inflict. He has violated the cartel." ,

"What has he done?" asked the Federal officer.

"He has taken possession of property left upon the field, contrary to the terms of the truce."

"Would you mind telling me," asked the Federal officer, "the exact nature and extent of his offence?"

A little explanation followed, the Confederate commander remaining stern and uncompromising in his determination to deliver the man for punishment, asking no favors or mercies for him, and offering no apologies for that which he deemed a breach of honor.

When the Federal officer had learned the exact facts of the situation, he made the usual military salute and said to the Confederate commander: "I thank you. You have been very honorable and very punctilious, but the officer's fault has been merely one of inadvertence. I beg to return him to you with the assurance that we have no desire to punish so brave a man as he must be, in order to hold his commission in your army, for an act that involved no intention of wrong."

Here were two brave men — two gentlemen — met. Naturally they understood each other.

OLD JONES AND THE HUCKSTER

IT is a fixed principle of military law that no person is allowed to sell supplies within the lines of a camp without permission of the commandant.

It is also a fixed principle of military law that he must sell only at prices approved by the commandant.

I shall never forget how I first learned of these military rules. We were at Camp Onward and old Jones had just become our colonel.

One day a farmer came to the camp with a heavily laden wagon. It was in the summer of 1861, when food in Northern Virginia was abundant, and when our money was as good as anybody's.

Our farmer had among his supplies, dressed turkeys, suckling pigs, lamb, mutton, watermelons, cantaloupes, string beans, Lima beans, green peas, and in brief almost all those things that we read about on the bill of fare of a swagger hotel, kept on the "American Plan."

He had butter also, and lard. He had eggplants and pumpkins, and a great many other things.

We were a rather hungry lot, and were strongly inclined to buy of him.

But this farmer had evidently made up his mind to get comfortably rich off that single wagon load of provisions. Two years later we should not have been surprised at his prices, but at that time we were appalled. Nevertheless, some of us were buying with the recklessness of men who do not know at what hour a bullet may draw a red line below all accounts.

Just then old Jones came out in his yellow coat and his pot hat, looking greatly more like a farmer than the wagon man did. Speaking through his nose, and with that extraordinary deliberation which always made his conversation a caricature of human speech, he asked: "What are you chargin' for turkeys? What are you chargin' for butter?" And so on through the list, receiving a reply to each query, and carefully noting it in his thoroughly organized mind.

Then he turned to one of the men and said: "Send the regimental commissary to me."

When the commissary came he said to him: "Take these supplies, and distribute them equitably among the different messes according to their numbers."

By this time the farmer had become alarmed. He said: "Who's goin' to pay for all this?"

"I am," said old Jones. "In my own way."

"Well, hold on," said the farmer.

"No, I reckon we won't hold on," said old Jones.

"But I'll send for the colonel of the regiment," said the farmer.

Then old Jones replied with a relish: "I am the colonel of this regiment. And I have ordered these food supplies distributed to the men in the messes. The regimental commissary will obey my orders. And as soon as your wagon is emptied, you will get out of this camp in a considerable of a hurry," — perhaps he used a shorter word than "considerable," — "or I'll hang you in front of headquarters. There's no court of appeals in this camp. Now git!" as the last of the supplies were taken out of the wagon by the regimental commissary.

We were all a little bit sorry that the poor farmer should lose his entire load. And yet we sympathized with old Jones's remark as he walked away.

"I'll teach these thieves that they can't loot a camp that I'm a runnin'."

A DEAD MAN'S MESSAGE

DICK FULCHER was the best natured man in the battery, and he was nothing else.

He was entirely ignorant and entirely content to be so. He could neither read nor write, and we could never persuade him to try to learn. He had nothing resembling pride in his composition apparently, nothing that it would do to call a character.

One morning the alarm came that the enemy had landed below, and we were ordered hurriedly forward. Fulcher had just taken post as stable-guard, and was, therefore, under no obligation of duty to go. He quietly threw down the musket he was carrying, and, going up to the sergeant-major, said: "Major, can't I be taken off guard? I want to go with the battery into the fight."

His request was granted, of course. He was number four at Joe's gun; number four is the man who pulls the lanyard, or string, that fires the gun. When we unlimbered to the front on Yemassee Creek, within pistol-shot range of the advancing enemy, Fulcher was laughing as usual, and apparently as indifferent to the work he was doing as he had been to everything else, since we had first known him.

I remember wondering, as I watched him, why a man who felt so little interest in the dangerous business had gone out of his way as he had done to engage in it.

The fire of the enemy was terrific in its destructiveness from the first. Within the first three minutes we had lost ten men and a score of horses. Among the men was Fulcher. He had fallen, shot through the body, just as the command was given to him to "fire."

Lying there upon the ground, with his life ebbing away, he made a feeble effort to pull the lanyard; but his strength was too far gone, and Joe, being short of men, took his place. He had to stand astride the poor dying fellow, in order to do his work, for Fulcher's wound was beyond the possibility of a surgeon's help.

After two or three more shots of the gun, Joe heard Fulcher feebly calling to him: "Joe — Joe." Inclining his ear, Joe received this last message: "I'm done for, sergeant. But won't you just write to my father and tell him I died like a man? I'd like him to know that about his only boy."

Joe wrote the letter and it was blotted with tears.

After all, it is hard to guess what a man is made of till you know his motives.

A Dead Man's Message.

A WOMAN'S LAST WORD

THE city of Richmond was in flames. We were beginning that last terrible retreat which ended the war. Fire had been set to the arsenal as a military possession, which must on no account fall into the enemy's hands.

As the flames spread, because of a turn of the wind, other buildings caught. The whole business part of the city was on fire. To make things worse, some idiot had ordered that all the liquor in the city should be poured into the gutters.

The rivers of alcohol had been ignited from the burning buildings, and in their turn had set fire to other buildings. It was a time and a scene of unutterable terror.

As we marched up the fire-lined street, with the flames scorching the very hair off our horses, George Goodsmith — the best cannoneer that ever wielded a rammer — came up to the headquarters squad, and said: "Captain, my wife's in Richmond. We've been married less than a year. She is soon to become a mother. I beg permission to bid her goodby. I'll join the battery later."

The permission was granted readily, and George Goodsmith put spurs to his horse. He had just been made a sergeant, and was therefore mounted.

It was in the gray of the morning that he hurriedly met his wife. With caresses of the tenderest kind, he bade her farewell. Realizing for a moment the utter hopelessness of our making another stand on the Roanoke, or any other line, he said in bitterness of soul: "Why shouldn't I stay here and take care of you?"

The woman straightened herself and replied: "I would rather be the widow of a brave man than the wife of a coward."

That was their parting, for the time was very short. Mayo's bridge across the James River was already in flames when Goodsmith perilously galloped across it.

Three or four days later, for I never could keep tab on time at that period of the war, we went into the battle at Farmville. Goodsmith was in his place in command of the piece.

Just before fire opened he beckoned to me and I rode up to hear what he had to say.

"I'm going to be killed, I think," he said. "If I am, I want my wife to know that she is the widow of a — *brave man*. I want her to know that I did my duty to the last. And — and if you live long enough, and this thing don't kill Mary — I want you to tell the *little one* about his father."

Goodsmith's premonition of his death was one of many that were fulfilled during the war.

A moment later a fearful struggle began. At the first fire George Goodsmith's wife became the "widow of a brave man." His body was heavy with lead.

His son, then unborn, is now a successful broker in a great city. There is nothing particularly knightly or heroic about him, for this is not a knightly or heroic age. But he takes very tender care of his mother — that "widow of a brave man."

AN INCOMPLETE STORY

WHEN General Field came to Cairo, Illinois, after the war, I welcomed him with especial heartiness.

I was a little bit lonely, lacking comrades in sympathy with me.

General Field had been my drillmaster at Ashland, at the war's beginning. Later, after he became a great general, I had many times been of his following in raids and scouts, and other military expeditions.

Like all the rest of us at the end of the war, General Field was very poor. He had come to Cairo to engage in business, and had not been able to bring his family with him. So he rented a bachelor room in the bank building in which my office was situated, and we two used to spend the evenings together in front of my office fire.

At that time General Don Carlos Buell was operating a coal mine in Kentucky, some distance up the Ohio River. He sold his coal through the commission house for which I was attorney.

When he came to Cairo, he, also, usually spent his evenings in my office.

One evening General Field was smoking a long pipe before my fire, and he and I were chatting about war times — we hadn't yet got far enough away from the war to regard any other topic as worthy of intelligent conversation.

"The saddest part of it all, to us of the old army at least," said General Field, "is the breaking up of old friendships. There's Buell, now. He and I once tented together, messed together, slept under the same blankets together, and, without any blankets at all, under the same frozen sky; marched together, fought together, suffered together, and endured together. Once we thought of each other as brothers might. Now, if we should meet, he would refuse even to shake my hand. He would regard me as a rebel — to him *anathema maranatha.*"

At this moment came a knock at the door. I opened it, and to my consternation there stood General Buell.

My first impulse was to say to him that I was overengaged that evening, and couldn't see him. My second was to invite him to my bedroom for a special conference, for which I could profess to have been longing. My third was to fabricate the story of a telegram, which should call him immediately to the house of the head of the firm.

Feeling that none of these devices would answer the purpose, I thought of the coal-shed below; but I remembered that there was no gas-burner there, and the night was rather a dark one.

Meantime, General Buell was catching cold in the hall. So at last I invited him in, taking pains to call him only by his title, not mentioning his name. As he entered, Field, who was always scrupulous in attention to the little niceties of courtesy, arose to receive the stranger.

When the two gentlemen had bowed to each other, — for it was no part of my purpose to introduce them, if I could help it, — I turned to General Buell and said: "General, I'm afraid there is a little discrepancy in the measurement of those last coal barges. If you have your memorandum book with you, we'll go to the outer office and straighten the thing up. The book-keepers are bothered about it."

Alas! My little device came to nothing. Buell had caught sight of Field, and Field had looked upon Buell. Though years of hard campaigning had intervened since they had last met, each recognized the other instantly, and after a moment's hesitation each threw himself into the other's arms.

"Why, it's Buell!"

"Why, it's Field!"

I can't tell the rest of this story, because I didn't stay to see it. I don't like to see two men hugging each other with tears in their eyes.

RANDOM FACTS

ILLUSTRATIVE OF SOUTHERN SOLDIER CONDITIONS

WE soldiers of the Southern army lacked many things. Sometimes we lacked almost everything. We did not always have clothes, but when we had any, they were apt to be good ones; they were made of cadet gray cloth, imported from England through the blockade. And those Englishmen have a habit of making uncommonly good cloths.

We were often without shoes; but when we had shoes, they also came from England, and were thoroughly good, both in material and make.

But towards the end of the war, we lacked many essential things. We lacked medicines for one thing, and quinine, especially. I remember that one gentlewoman was deemed a peculiar patriot, because she got through the lines with one hundred and forty ounce bottles of quinine hung inside her hoop-skirt.

For lack of that and other drugs, our surgeons had to resort to many substitutions.

Some of these were discoveries of permanent value. That is why the medical profession has studied with interest the records of our Southern surgeon-general's department, now in possession of the war department at Washington.

These records, it is said, contribute more than any other like documents to the science of medicine.

Another thing that we terribly lacked was gunpowder — the one supreme agent of all warfare. Our fire was often compulsorily made as light as possible, in order to spare our cartridge boxes.

To supply this rudimentary need, the women of the country diligently dug up the earthen floors of all their smokehouses, and all their tobacco barns, and rendered out the nitre they contained. Some of them even destroyed their tobacco crops by boiling, in order to extract the precious salt necessary to the destruction of their enemy.

In the cities, our womenkind were requested to preserve and deliver to government collectors all those slops that contain nitre.

It was in this way alone that we got gunpowder enough to maintain resistance to the end. And we had equally to pinch in other ways in order that we might continue to be "fighting men."

All the window-weights in all the houses, and

all the other leaden things that could be melted down, were converted into bullets. Even then we ran dreadfully short towards the end of the war. At Petersburg, good soldiers felt it to be their duty to spend all their spare time in collecting the multitudinous bullets with which the ground was everywhere strewn. These battered missiles turned into the arsenals were remoulded and came back to us in the form of effective, fixed ammunition.

When we marched to meet Grant in the Wilderness, in the spring of 1864, we were about the most destitute army that ever marched to meet anybody, anywhere. We had nothing to transport, and we had no transportation.

At the beginning of every campaign it is customary for the commanding general to issue an order, setting forth the allotment of baggage wagons to officers and men. Just before we marched that spring some wag in the army had printed and circulated a mock order from General Lee, a copy of which now lies before me.

GENERAL ORDERS, NUMBER 1.
HEADQUARTERS, ARMY OF NORTHERN VIRGINIA,
April 20, 1864.

The allotment of baggage wagons to the officers and men of the Army of Northern Virginia during the coming campaign will be as follows: —

To every thirty officers . . . No baggage wagon.
To every three hundred men . . . Ditto.

(Signed) ROBERT E. LEE, General.

This order was a good-natured forgery, of course. Nevertheless it was carried out to the letter. The fact is that we had no baggage and no baggage wagons. The only baggage wagons I ever heard of in connection with that campaign were a few that General D. H. Hill summoned for a special occasion. His musicians put in a petition at the beginning of the summer's work for wagons to carry their instruments. He assented instantly, and ordered the wagons brought up. As soon as the instruments were comfortably deposited within them, he turned to his quartermaster and said: "Send those wagons to Richmond." Then turning to his adjutant he said: "Have muskets issued to these men immediately."

General D. H. Hill was not a man from whose orders anybody under him was disposed to appeal.

We entered that campaign stripped almost to the buff. We had no tents, even for the highest officers. We had no canteens. We had no haversacks. We had no knapsacks. We had no oilcloths to sleep on. We had no tin cups. We had almost no cooking utensils and almost no blankets. We had no shoes, and our socks had long ago been worn out. We had an average of one overcoat to every thousand men.

It was in this condition of destitution that we entered the battles in the Wilderness. The

Federal army was as much oversupplied as we were underfurnished with all the necessaries of campaigning. What with a perfectly equipped quartermaster's department, a sanitary commission volunteering superfluous tin cups and everything else and with other sources of lavish supply, public and private, every Federal soldier entered the campaign carrying about three times as much as any soldier should carry. The moment there was fighting to be done, they shed all these things — as a man throws off his overcoat when there is work to do.

In the shiftings and changes of position that occurred during that most irregular of all possible contests, we were thrown often into positions where the shedding had been done. The first thought of every man of us was to equip himself with such necessaries as were lying about. It took us a week to get rid of the superfluous plunder, and reduce ourselves again to the condition of soldiers in light marching order.

The one worst lack of all we could not supply in this way. That was the lack of food. It was an army of starving men that fought those battles in the Wilderness. It was an army of starving men that confronted Grant at Spottsylvania. It was an army of starving men that faced the guns at Cold Harbor, at Bottom's bridge, and all the way to Petersburg. Not until we were established in the works there, did any man have enough food in a week to supply his physical needs for a day. I have elsewhere in these stories illustrated this fact somewhat, but as it was the central fact in connection with that campaign, it seems to me important here to state it in its fulness.

At Petersburg we began to get something like regular rations, though they were very meagre and of extremely bad quality. It was, perhaps, under the influence of this prolonged starvation and hard work that the men fell victims to the great religious revival of that time. It was the ecstasy of anchorites. It proved, if anything ever did, the efficacy of fasting as an inducement to fervid prayer. Saint Simeon Stylites perched on top of his tower was no better subject of religious enthusiasm than were these worn out and starved veterans, whose cause was an object of perpetual worship. They believed no longer in themselves; they no longer looked even to their generals for results. The time and the mood had come when they trusted God alone to give them victory. Starvation had made them devotees.

MY FRIEND PHIL[1]

To begin with, Phil was black. The reader will please understand that the word "black" is here used in its literal, and not in its conventional, sense. Phil was actually as well as ethnologically black. There was no trace of a lighter tint anywhere in his complexion. Not a suspicion of brown appeared in his cheeks, and even his great thick lips, protruding far beyond the outposts of his nose, were as sable as the rest of his face. It was all a dead black, too, unaccompanied by that lustre which, by surface reflection, relieves the shadow upon commonplace African faces.

And nobody knew all this better than Phil did.

"Phil ain't none o' yer coffee-colored niggas," he would say in moments of exultation, when his mood was to straighten his broad shoulders and boast a little. "Phil ain't none o' yer coffee-colored niggas, ner none o' yer *alapacker*

[1] This story was first printed in the *Galaxy* for December, 1875. It is here reprinted by courteous permission of Colonel William Conant Church, now of the *Army and Navy Journal*, under whose editorship the *Galaxy* was made a conspicuous and honorable factor in American literature.

niggas, nuther. Ise black, I is. Dat's sho'. Ain't got no bacon-rind shine in *my* skin; but I jes' tell yer what, mastah, Phil kin jes' take the very shut offen dem shiny niggas an' hoff an' hoff niggas, when 't comes to de wuk. Drive? Kin I? Kin Phil drive? What yer mean, mastah, by axin' such a question?"

Nobody had asked Phil such a question; but Phil had some remarks that he wanted to make on the subject of his accomplishments in this respect, and was disposed to answer what he wished somebody would ask.

"Drive? Co'se I kin. Der never was a hoss ner mule yit whatever had a mouf an' two laigs dat Phil can't han'le, an' yer better b'lieve, mastah, Phil can plaunt de wheel 'twix' de acorn an' de shell."

If I report Phil's boastings, it is only because they constitute too large a proportion of what he said to be omitted. I do so to confirm, not to gainsay them, or to hold their author up to ridicule.

He was my friend, the faithfulest one I ever knew, and now he is dead.

If he boasted now and then, no one could have had a better right. His was the pride of performance, and not the vanity of pretension.

Phil was a Virginian — and a gentleman in his way — and a slave, though I doubt if he ever suspected his gentility, or felt his bondage as a burden in the least. He had no aspirations for freedom or for anything else, I think, except jollity and comfort. I do not say that this was well, but it was a fact.

My acquaintance with Phil began when I was a half-grown boy. Until that time I had lived in a free state, so that when I had returned to the land of my fathers, and become an inmate of the old family mansion in one of the south-side counties of Virginia, the plantation negro was a fresh and very interesting study to me.

On the morning after my arrival, as I lay in the antique carved bed assigned to me, wondering at the quaint picturesqueness of my surroundings, and the delightful strangeness of the life which I was now in contact with for the first time, a weird, musical sound, of singular power and marvellous sweetness, floated through the open dormer windows, borne upon the breath of such a June morning as I had never before seen. I listened, but could make nothing of it by guessing. It was music, certainly, at least a "concord of sweet sounds." It rose and fell like the ground swell of the sea, and was as full of melody and sweetness as is the song of birds, but it was as destitute as they of anything like a tune. It began nowhere, and went nowhither. I had no memory of anything with which to compare it, and could conceive of no throat or instrument capable of producing such a sound.

On the great piazza below, at the front of the house, sat the master of the mansion. Of him I straightway made inquiry.

"What is that?" I asked curiously.

"Phil," answered my uncle.

"And who is 'Phil,' and what on earth is he doing, and especially how is he doing it?"

"He is calling the hogs, and you may be sure he is doing it well. If you'll walk up to that skirt of woods, you can put your other questions to him in person. He is not shy or difficult of approach. Introduce yourself — be sure to tell him whose son you are."

My uncle's face wore an amused smile as I walked away. He could imagine the sequel.

In the edge of the timber stood a tall, broad-shouldered, brawny negro man. He was singularly ugly, but with a countenance so full of good humor that I was irresistibly attracted by it from the first. At his feet stood great baskets of corn, and around him were gathered a hundred or more swine, busily eating the breakfast he was dispensing. As I approached, his hat — what there was of it — was doffed. I was greeted with a fabulous bow, apparently meant to be half a tribute of respect, and half a bit of buffoonery, indulged in for my amusement or his own.

"Good mawnin', young mastah. I hope I see you well dis mawnin'."

"Thank you, I'm very well," I replied. "You're Phil, I suppose?"

"You're right, fo' dis wunst, young mastah. Ise Phil toe be sho'. Ax der hawgs—dey done know me."

"Well, Phil, I'm glad to make your acquaintance. I'm your mas' Jo's son."

"What dat? Mas' Jo's son! Mas' Jo's son!! MY MAS' JO'S SON!!! Lem me shake han's wid you, mastah. Jes' to think! Mas' Jo's son! An' Phil done live to shake han's wid mas' Jo's son. Why, my young mastah, I done raise your father! Him an' me done play ma'bles togeder many and many a time. We was boys togeder right heah, on dis very identumcal plauntation. Used to go in swimmin' togeder, an' go fishin' an' steal de mules out'n de stables Sundays, an' ride races wid 'em and git cotched, too, sometimes when ole mastah git home from chu'ch. My Mastah. But Ise glad to see yer."

All this while the great giant was wrenching my hand well-nigh off, laughing and weeping alternately, and stamping with a delight which could find no other vent than in physical exertion. I was naturally anxious to divert the conversation into some other and less personal channel, and managed to do so presently by asking Phil to give me a specimen of his hog-calling cry, which I wished to hear near at hand.

That performance over, we talked again. I began by saying I had never heard any one call hogs in that way before.

"Dat's jes' it, mastah," he replied. "Folks don't understan' de *science* o' hog-callin'. Dey says ' p-o-o-o-o-o-o-o-r 'og,' when de hogs ain't po' at all, but fat as buttah. Dey got to git 'hog' in some ways so dey thinks. But dey ain't no sense in dat. Hogs don't understan' dat. Dey can't talk an' don't understan' de meanin' o' talk words. You mus' jes' let 'em know dat when you wants 'em to come youse gwine to make a noise, de like o' which ain't in heaven or yuth. Den dey gits to knowin' what dat means. Dat's my way. When I fetch a yell at 'em, dey jes' raise der yeahs, an' say to der se'f: 'Dat dar's Phil, fo' sho', an' Phil's de big, ugly, black nigga wid de bauskets o' cawn.' When you says 'Phil,' you mean mastah's big nigga what wuks in de fiel', an' plays de banjo, an' goes fishin'; but when de hogs says 'Phil,' dey mean a big black fella, wid a big yell into him, *an'* de bauskets o' cawn. An' you bettah b'lieve dat makes 'em jump up an' clap dey han's fo' joy, jes' like de nigga does when he gets religion 'nuff to make him shout, an' *not* 'nuff to keep him offen the hen roos's. If a nigga gits 'nuff religion to keep him from stealin', it's a mistake. Dey don't never mean to do it, and when dey does, dey ain't glad a bit, an' dey hurries up an' sends de surplage back."

Phil's respect for what he called "niggas" was exceedingly small, and it was his greatest pleasure in life to demonstrate their inferiority and emphasize their shortcomings in a hundred ways.

He was "head man" of the hoe hands — which is to say he hoed the leading row of tobacco hills, and was charged with the duty of superintending the work of the others. It was his delight to keep his work so far in advance that he must now and then set his hoe in the ground, and walk back to inspect the progress, and criticise the performance of slower workers than he. In all this there was no spice of uncharitableness or malice, however. He wished his fellows well, and had no desire to hurt their feelings; but he keenly enjoyed the fun of outdoing them, and laughing at their inability to cope with him.

It was during wheat harvest, however, that Phil was in his full glory. The rapidity with which he could "cradle" wheat was a matter of astonishment to every one who knew him, and, what was more wonderful still, he was able to maintain a distinctly "spurting" speed all day and every day.

"Phil," his master would say, as the men entered the field on the first day, "I want no racing now; it's too hot."

"Now you heah dat, you slow niggas! Mastah says Phil mustn't kill his niggas, an' de onliest way to save yo' lives is fer yer not to try to follow me. Jes' take yo' time, boys. Race a little among yo'selves, if yer want to, but don' yer try to get a look at de heels o' my boots, if yer don' want to go to de bushes an' has any intrus' in mastah."

A negro, exhausting himself in a race, lies down in the bushes to cool off and recuperate, and hence the winner of the race is said to send the others "to the bushes."

Phil's preliminary remarks were sure to exasperate his fellows and put them on their mettle. Silently they would determine to "push" him, and the utmost vigilance of the master was taxed to prevent dangerous overexertion. If the reapers were left alone for half an hour, several of them would be sure to overtask their strength, and retire exhausted to the friendly shade of the nearest thicket. But they never succeeded in coming up with Phil, or in so tiring him that he was not ready for a dance or a tramp when night came.

He was a strong man, rejoicing in his strength always; but there was one thing he would not do — he would not work for himself.

His master was one of those who hoped for gradual emancipation, as many Virginians did, and thought it his duty to prepare his negroes for freedom, so far as it was possible for him to do so. Among other means to this end, he encouraged each to make and save money on his own account. Each was expected to cultivate a "patch" of his own. Their master gave them the necessary time and the use of the mules whenever their crops needed attention.

In this way he thought to train them in habits of voluntary industry and thrift; and some of them, having no necessary expenses to bear, accumulated very pretty little hoards of cash from the sale of their crops every year. But Phil would not raise a crop for himself.

"What I want to raise a crop for?" he would ask. "I don' want no money, on'y a quarter sometimes to buy a banjo string or a fish line, an' I get plenty o' quarters pitched at me when I hol' de gentlemen's hosses. I don' want no money, an' I wouldn't know what to do wid it if I had it. My mastah takes good care o' me, an 's long as dar's a piece o' meat in de smokehouse, Phil knows he's gwine to have plenty to eat. I ain't gwine to earn no money an' be cas'in' 'flections on my mastah. My mastah gives me mo' clo'es 'an I kin war out; an' *what de devil* I want to be makin' money for, I donno."

It was of no use to argue the matter. His

mind was quite made up, and there was no possibility of changing it.

Phil's marital philosophy was unique. He changed wives half a dozen times while I knew him, but one set of rules governed his choice in every instance. There were certain qualifications of a rather singular sort, which he deemed essential in a wife. She must not live on the plantation for one thing, or on one of those immediately adjoining, "'Cause den we're sho' to see too much o' one anoder, an' 'll git tired o' de 'rangement." In the second place he would marry none but *old* women, "'Cause de young ones is no 'count anyway. Dey don' half take car' o' dey husban's stockin's and things. 'F you want holes in yer stockin's an' buttons off yer shut collahs, jes' you marry a young gal." The third requisite was that the wife should be a slave, and the daughter of slaves on both sides. This qualification he insisted upon, even in the choice of masculine associates. His contempt for "free niggas" was supreme, almost sublime. He neglected no possible opportunity of villifying them, and practised no sort of economy in his expenditure of invective upon them.

Most of the negroes — in Virginia, at least — were very religious. Naturally their religion was intensely emotional in its character, — ecstatic, sombre, gloomy, — and quite as naturally it was largely colored with superstition. But religion of this kind had no charm for Phil, who, as the reader may possibly have guessed, prided himself on being strictly logical in all his views and actions.

"Bro' Ben," he said to one of his fellows one day, "youse done got religion, I heah. Anyway, your face is twict as long as it ought to be. Has yer got religion fo' sho'?"

"Now, Phil, I don't want none o' your wickedness. Bless de Lord, Ise *got* religion."

"Oh, you *is* got it, is you? Now lemme ax yer a question or two. Youse got religion, yer say?"

Ben: "Yes, Ise got religion."

Phil: "Well, den, you're gwine to heaven after while — when yer dies?"

Ben: "Yes, Ise got de 'surance o' dat, bro' Phil."

Phil: "An' you'd 'a' gone to hell, if you hadn't got de 'surance, as you calls it, wouldn't you?"

Ben: "If I'd 'a' died in my sins, course I'd 'a' gone to hell."

Phil: "Well now fo' a nigga what's jes' made his 'rangements to keep out'n hell an' git into heaven, youse got de mos' onaccountable long face I ever did see, an' dat's all about it."

When Ben had retired in disgust, I remonstrated with Phil.

"What do you tease Ben for, Phil?" I asked. "You know better than to make fun of religion."

"Course I do, mastah, an' dat's jes' it. Ben ain't got no religion, an' I knows it. He's jes' puttin' on dat solemncholy face to fool de good Lord wid. Ben'll steal, mastah, whenever he gits a chaunce. He ain't got no mo' religion 'n a hog. Sho. What he know 'bout religion, goin' down under de hill to pray, an' all dat nonsense? Couldn't git him to sing a song or whistle a tune now on no account whatsumever, but he ain't no better nigga for dat. Didn't I see? He shouted mighty loud las' night, but he shu'ked his wuk dis mawnin' an' didn't half curry his mules; an' religion dat don't make a nigga take good car' o' po' dumb creeters like mules ain't wuth nuthin' at all, no way yo' kin fix it. When dey keeps de row up jes' a little better, an' don't cover up no weeds dey ought to cut down, an' takes good car' o' mules, an' quits stealin', den I begins to 'spect 'em o' havin' de real religion. But dey can't fool Phil wid none o' dere sham solemncholies."

Phil was a trifle hard and uncharitable, perhaps, in his judgments upon his fellows in a matter of this kind; but there was, at any rate, no hypocrisy in his composition. And what is more singular still, I was never able to discover any trace of superstition in his conduct. He laughed to scorn the signs and omens with which the other negroes were perpetually encouraged or affrighted. Friday was as lucky a day as any in his calendar. He would even make his fire with the wood of a lightning-riven tree, and stranger still, was not afraid, as all the rest were, on the occasion of a funeral, to bring away the shovels used in the church-yard, without waiting till the moon and stars had shone upon them.

"How is it, Phil," I once asked him, "that you don't believe in any of the luck signs?"

"Do you b'lieve in 'em, mastah?" he asked in reply.

"No, of course not, but all the black folks do, except you."

"Mastah, ain't you foun' out yit dat niggas is bawn fools? When my mastah wants de hogs changed from one piece o' woods to annuder, he don't go to makin' blin' signs to me, but he comes an' tells me what he wants; an' de good Lord what made de wuld, he ain't a-goin' to make no blin' signs, nuther. He's done tole us in de good book an' in all de wuld aroun' us what to do. He's put sense in our heads to un'erstan' what he means, an' he ain't gwine to govern de univarse wid a lot o' luck signs, like a nigga would do it. 'Sides, Ise done all de unlucky things heaps o' times, an' ain't never had no bad luck yit."

When the war came, Phil was a stanch

Southerner in all his feeling, and firmly held to his faith in the success of his side, even to the end. The end crushed him completely. When his master explained to the colored people their new condition of freedom, and proposed to engage them for wages, Phil stoutly refused.

"De odder folks may do as dey pleases, mastah, but Phil's gwine to be your nigga jes' as he always was. I ain't gwine to be free nohow. I ain't got no free nigga blood in me. I never saw no free nigga what wasn't hungry; an' I don't know no free nigga what *won't steal;* more'n dat, I never know'd a free nigga what wouldn't sneak up on birds an' *shoot 'em on de groun'*. I tell you, I ain't gwine to be no sich folks as dem. Ise your nigga, an' Ise gwine to be jes' dat. I'll do my wuk, an' I ain't goin' to take no wages, an' you'll take car' o' me jes' as you always did, on'y don't never call me no free nigga. Ise a slave, I is, an' Ise got de bes' mastah in ole Virginy, an' I ain't fool 'nough to want to change de sitiwation."

His master explained to him the necessity of the case, and showed him how impossible it was, by any mutual agreement, to alter the fact of freedom, or to escape its consequences.

"You must accept wages, Phil, for I may die or go into bankruptcy, and you may grow old or get ill; and if I should be poor or dead, then there would be nobody to take care of you. You must work for wages and take care of your money, so that it may take care of you."

"Mastah, do you mean to tell Phil dat de law makes me a free nigga whedder or no?"

"Yes, Phil."

"Den stick yo' fingers in yo' years, mastah, 'cause Ise gwine to swear. *Damn* de law. Dat's what I say about dat. An' now Ise jus' gwine to die, an' dat's all about it."

The poor fellow walked away with bowed head and tear-stained face. The broad, stalwart shoulders were bent beneath the weight of responsibility for himself. He was a strong man, physically, but the merest child in character, and the feeling that he no longer had any one but himself to lean upon, was more than he could bear. The light of cheerfulness and good humor went out of his face. The joyousness of his nature disappeared, and before the summer had ripened into autumn, poor Phil lay down and died of a broken heart.

www.ingramcontent.com/pod-product-compliance
Lightning Source LLC
Chambersburg PA
CBHW031951230426
43672CB00010B/2125